STORM FORCE

Also by the same author:

Braving the Storm (Authentic Media), 2007
Trust: Enduring Hope (Spring Harvest Publishing
and Authentic Media), 2006

STORM FORCE

Winning the battle for the mind

Eric Gaudion

Authentic

MILTON KEYNES ● COLORADO SPRINGS ● HYDERABAD

This edition published 2009 by Authentic Media
9 Holdom Avenue, Bletchley, Milton Keynes, MK1 1QR, UK
1820 Jet Stream Drive, Colorado Springs, CO 80921, USA
OM Authentic Media, Medchal Road, Jeedimetla Village,
Secunderabad 500 055, A.P., India
www.authenticmedia.co.uk

Authentic Media is a division of IBS-STL U.K., limited by guarantee, with its
Registered Office at Kingstown Broadway, Carlisle, Cumbria CA3 0HA.
Registered in England & Wales No. 1216232. Registered charity 270162

British Library Cataloguing in Publication Data
A catalogue record for this book is available from the British Library

ISBN-13: 978-1-85078-820-1

Cover Design by fourninezero design.
Print Management by Adare
Printed in Great Britain by J.H. Haynes & Co., Sparkford

When storm force winds blow and devastation threatens, you have few resources that really matter. Good warning, a place of safety and people who know how to help are among the best. I want to thank some of those who have been with me over the long-term in this storm. Diane, my lovely wife, and Matthew our son. Sandie and Ashley, and more recently Malcom Ward. Jim and Margery Dick, Tony Downes, Barbara Stanford, Brian and Doreen Rabey and all the wonderful folk at Shiloh Church, Guernsey. Thank you all.

Thanks, too, to my editor Alison Hull, and to Kath Williams and Mark Finnie at Authentic for encouraging me to write *Storm Force*.

Contents

Contents

Foreword

When you're ill, you need friends. They come bearing warm smiles, words of encouragement, and most importantly, grapes. I'm not sure if there is any medicinal benefit from grapes, but they certainly are a welcome sight when one is under the weather. And Lucozade was always a treat when I was a child, and not just because I thought that the glucose drink was named in my honour. Friends bearing gifts can help us through the coughs and sniffles, and bring sunshine during the rainy seasons when more serious illnesses smite us.

But not all well-meaning friends are helpful, as Job famously discovered when his so-called comforters showed up and were about as comforting as a rack in a torture chamber. Their skewed theology of suffering gave poor old Job an extra dose of pain. As if all those scabs and boils and funerals and financial melt-downs weren't enough to test his faith to the limit, he then had to deal with a pack of slogan-toting theological gunslingers who made his miserable life even worse with their advice.

And some of Job's friends linger. Terrible things are often said (by well-meaning Christian people) to those who suffer. One of the perennial favourites is the notion that because Christ went to the Cross for us, we are all automatically able to claim 'healing in the atonement'. Of course, Christians still get sick (and die) which is a problem for those who cling to this idea. Suddenly, the sufferer has an additional burden to their gammy leg, recurring headache or terminal cancer. Now, they stand accused, the indictment that they are lacking in faith an additional, crushing burden to bear.

This book comes as a welcome painkiller for all who suffer. Eric Gaudion has two earned doctorates – one in theology, and the other in faithfulness. He speaks to us, not from the isolated cloisters of theory, but from the school of hard knocks, where he has spent far too long. His daily battle with excruciating pain could have driven him into madness; instead, he speaks from that pain with a sanity that is a balm of authentic comfort. His warm words are better than any professional bedside manner.

God is not the author of evil and pain, but he is the redeemer of it; he brings beauty out of ugliness, and gold out of the furnace of agony. This book is a wonderful example of that redeeming work. May it soothe your brow, cheer your heart, and kiss you once more with genuine hope.

Jeff Lucas

The Heat is On

The ancient flatbed truck staggered up the hill ahead of me. Clouds of choking black fumes billowed out from its exhaust, thick enough to coat the front of my own vehicle with soot if I ventured too close. Creeping forward on the single track road gave me ample time to count the people crammed into the back, roof and cab of the ageing death-trap. There were two dozen people clinging on, plus goats, chickens cooped up in homemade wicker cages, piles of clothing bundles, small cases and buckets. On the roof of the cab perched a small child with its sibling, enjoying the ride. I could not see through the back window of the cab, but I was sure that every inch of the inside around the driver and the passenger spaces would be packed too. This was Africa, after all and although I had lived there for some time already, this sight still took me by surprise.

As we neared the brow of the hill, the groaning lorry's engine slowed in order to stop and collect more passengers. Hard as it was to believe, by Zimbabwean standards this public service vehicle still had room to spare! I eased past with my load of drought relief supplies for the rural mission hospital with which we were working as missionaries and shook my head at the wonders of

African ingenuity and the attitude of 'There's always room for more!'

The picture of the overloaded truck comes back to me a lot. After twelve years of pancreatitis, a deadly disease which gives some of the worst pain known to man, several operations, countless hospital admissions, spells in intensive care units and near death encounters, I have often felt the same way. Just when I thought that my back was crowded, every inch of my carrying capacity was spoken for and my ability to endure was strained to its limits, the driver decided to stop for more. What is even more surprising is that the Driver of my life is Jesus and I would have credited him with more sense. Doesn't he know that I'm at my limits? Can't he hear the creaking prayers of my aching engine as it struggles to crest one more brow on life's journey?

Such a picture is typical of those who are managing life with chronic pain and awaiting the Healer. The pain itself is a hard enough load to bear and stretches our resources thinly. On top of that comes all manner of other loads, some self-inflicted and others not. There have been many times during over more than a decade of agony, that I have shouted 'Enough! I can't cope with any more!' I knew as a Christian leader and pastor that God is supposed to work through our sufferings to change us and cause us to grow as people. It may sound cheeky to you, or even blasphemous, but I prayed 'Lord, I've done pain and suffering for a decade now. I think I've got the T-shirt. Can I please do something else in order to grow?'

What makes my journey into suffering particularly difficult to bear are the constant reminders along the way that a good number of Christians believe that I ought to be doing much better as a man of faith. Surely, they reason, sometimes out loud and occasionally in writing, God's will is to heal the sick, isn't it? And didn't Jesus die to carry all our sicknesses on the cross? I have received believing prayer in the name of Jesus from some of the biggest names in the healing ministry and in some of the world's revival hot-spots, where I had travelled specifically to be healed. Yet still I am ill. Others have been healed around me, even healed in response to my own and my church's ministry, but my condition remains the same. The trouble is that secretly, in my dark and lonely painful hours, I agree with them. The problem must surely be with me, I think. Doesn't the Bible say 'by his stripes we are healed'? I am not – so surely there must be something wrong with my faith? The occasional rebellious thought that there might be something amiss with God's plan for me, or lacking in his love for me, also surfaces. Sometimes it seems a lot easier to deny that there is even a God than to face the possibility that he is in some way conniving in my agony. I understand how tempting it must have been for Job to listen to his wife nagging him with 'Curse God and die!'

There can be some value in bearing heavy loads. I saw a television series recently which followed a young man training to become a Royal Marine Commando. On a forced march designed to cover ten miles in around forty minutes or so, he was ordered to carry a backpack weighing twenty kilos. When his pack was checked by the officers prior to setting out, it was found to be a few grams short, so he was sent off to pick up some stones to add to his burden – presumably as some kind of test. However, when the producers followed the young man through graduation and out to the battle-field in Afghanistan, I noticed that he was sent into fire-fights without his backpack whenever it was possible to do so. He could fight more freely without the load that he had been trained to bear. I suppose the moral of this tale is that there is a time to bear burdens and a time to be set free (Eccl. 3:1–18). When a soldier is in close contact with the enemy, it is not the time to load him down with extra weight. That would be like tying one hand behind his back. If he is to be successful in the fight, he needs to be as light as possible. The time to bear the weight is in training – so maybe I am in training for some great mission. I hope so, because it would be such an added sorrow if all this pain were for nothing.

Getting rid of the excess

I have written this book on the subject of healing, along with its predecessor *Braving the Storm*, to try and ease the loads that suffering people have to carry. It's not that I want to excuse you from necessary training, for that would be doing you no favours. But I believe many of us are carrying our packs right into battle. Just when we should be free to fight the great fight of faith, we are struggling to believe under a load of condemnation. That can't be right. I want to talk to sufferers directly to try to help them identify ways in which they can get rid of unnecessary burdens on their road to recovery, or even so that they can hang in there during tough times. They need to be equipped to fight suffering on all fronts: physical, emotional and spiritual. My words are also addressed to those who love and support people in pain, because it is all too easy to miss those occasions when what we are doing with all good intent adds to the problem rather than solving it. I want to plead with pastors and leaders in my own Christian tradition to ask that we stop placing burdens which are far too heavy on the backs of the already vulnerable. We sometimes do this unwittingly through our preaching and teaching, but also in our public praying and casual conversation if we are not careful. Jesus once responded to questions raised by the Scribes and Pharisees with the words, 'And you experts in the law, woe to you, because you load people down with burdens they can hardly carry and you yourselves will not lift one finger to help them' (Lk. 11:46). When Paul was telling the Galatians how they should treat one another, despite the theological divisions that were between them, he urged: 'Carry each other's burdens and in this way you will fulfil the law of Christ' (Gal. 6:2).

Why this matters so much

Recent changes to luggage regulations on low cost airlines mean that a lot of us are learning to travel with a lot less baggage than we used to. I think that is a good thing because the less you pack, the less you have to heave around. We have started to prioritise – do I need this or is it just adding unnecessary weight?

God never intended us to carry the kind of loads we usually stagger about under today. Some of them are inflicted on us by well meaning fellow travellers but we don't need them. If we are struggling with illness, distress or pain, we already have enough to carry without these extra burdens. When adversity does strike, we don't have space for anything but the bare essentials of survival. So for the sake of our loved ones – as well as for our own sakes – let's ditch any unnecessary loads and learn to travel light. As Max Lucado says: 'Travelling light means trusting God with the burdens you were never intended to bear.'[1]

The internal load

One of these unwanted loads could be called internal. In the early days of my illness, a big part of coping was what was going on in my mind, not just in my body. Throughout my pain, there were occasions when tests came back negative and scans revealed little or nothing wrong. I presumed that the problem must be in my imagination. Others hinted at the same idea, including certain confused doctors and even consultants and yet I know now that all that time I was battling a deadly disease that takes the lives of a high percentage of sufferers in this country every year. But even if it had all been 'in my mind' as I thought, mental pain is very real and often underestimated especially in Christian circles.

A retired consultant psychiatrist and good friend of mine, Professor David Enoch has said: 'Christians who suffer from mental illness find it particularly difficult to accept, are often bewildered and baffled by their condition and accompanying this there may be a feeling of guilt.'[2] He criticises those who aggravate this (including pastors and clergy) by clearly indicating that they have no time for psychiatry and psychiatrists. Indeed, some have even suggested that psychiatry is 'of the devil.' What an unnecessary and unhelpful load to place upon the backs of sufferers who are using every means at their disposal to overcome the most appalling pressures.

I intend to show that wherever the problem is centred, there is a battle going on in our minds in which we need all the help we can get. It is in our emotions and our beliefs that we often win or lose the battle for our survival. When pain wracks the body, what happens in the mind is even more critical. We take drugs to alleviate pain but they can have side effects on our feelings. We spend time resting in order to recover our strength but then find that the very rest has been negative in emotional terms, as we have had too much time to think. Occasionally, there is space to prepare for the storm in advance. The early chapters in Part One will address the question of how we can be best prepared to overcome in the battle of the mind.

The theological load

An even more difficult burden to bear when the chips are down is the theological load of guilt and condemnation. It was early in the morning, long before breakfast, but Diane and I had been up all night. We were longing for the dawn to come, as you do when you are ill and the nights seem so long. As soon as it was decent, Diane phoned a close colleague and pastor friend who we knew prayed for us often and who said that he believed God for my healing. Perhaps it was the early hour that caused him to be short with Diane on the phone, but it was hard for an exhausted carer to receive a theological lecture that morning.

'Don't you realise, Diane, that it was all done for you two thousand years ago on the cross?'

'Well yes,' she replied nervously, her tired mind searching for the right words to say, 'I know Jesus died for us but we have had such a terrible night and I wondered if you would say a prayer for us now?'

'When will you stop this unbelief and start trusting in what God has already done for you? Claim your rights and be healed in Jesus' name!'

'Yes, we'll do our best.'

And he was a close friend and colleague! He meant well, but his theology was skewed. It resulted in him laying upon us a burden that we were not strong enough to bear.

Certain teachings have crept into the Pentecostal and Charismatic movement churches that have added to the loads of suffering individuals rather than easing them. One such is the teaching that physical healing is available in the atonement – that is the death of Jesus Christ on the cross – on the same basis as forgiveness of sins. This develops into the claim that there is a legally binding agreement by God to heal all those who believe. If this teaching is mistaken, however, then a very cruel trick is being played on the minds of people already battling for the survival of their faith. Instead of looking hopefully towards a compassionate, healing God, who is also a sovereign and sustaining Father in their hour of need, they are led to believe that there is a legal transaction that was put into effect two thousand years ago. Try as they might, for many it doesn't seem possible to enter into the good of it and they end up doubting their own salvation.

It is in order to correct that misunderstanding that I have written Parts Two and Three of this book. They will offer us the opportunity to go the Scriptures and to see another way of understanding the Bible verses that are often misused in support of this teaching. I hope that doing so will set us free from the burdens of self-condemnation, failure and guilt with which so many Christians who believe in divine healing afflict themselves. These chapters will present a theology of suffering where God is still at work in our lives when things are toughest. Above all, they will open our eyes to the love of a caring heavenly Father who does not give up on his children when they are ill, or in failure or disaster, but who draws near to them at such times and wants them to know his healing presence. In fact, God likes us. When grappling with the enemy on all fronts, that is very good to know.

Part One

The Battle For the Mind

Part One

The Battle for the Mind

Chapter 1

Be Transformed . . .

During the second Gulf War in 2003 the first wave of coalition force attacks sent in to Iraq were designed to knock out the Iraqi command and control systems and to disrupt their communications. The reasoning was that if orders could not get through to the humble foot soldiers then they would be leaderless and more likely to surrender. The tactic was also designed to forestall the release of the deadly 'weapons of mass destruction' which, it was wrongly believed, were ready to be launched.

The mind is the body's control and command centre, from where the communication network of the nervous system originates. That's why it matters so much that we focus on the battle for the mind at the beginning of this survival manual.

I find that the pressure on my mind caused by constant pain is not alleviated by drugs. Most of the drugs that I need in order to cope with overwhelming pain have a negative effect on the mind. I didn't expect this to be the case. After all, if pain is relieved I imagined that the mind would be at rest. And don't some people take opiates and other pain killers to get high? I have needed morphine, Fentanyl (a form of synthetic morphine said to be eighty to one hundred times as strong as morphine) and the medical form of heroin. It has certainly not made me high and thankfully I have avoided becoming addicted to it. More often than not it makes me depressed. Perhaps it's the guilt at having to take it at all. Maybe it has a depressing effect on my mood. Whatever, the outcome is that I fight the worst battles on the battlefield of my mind and I think that a few fellow-sufferers do so too.

In military campaigns there is a period during which forces can prepare for the conflict ahead. That's how it was in both Gulf Wars. Troops, equipment, resources and materials were all stockpiled in advance so that the battle itself would be effective. Sometimes there is even time to prepare in advance of the moment of the attack on the battlefield itself. You may not be in the grip of the fog of war at the moment, but now is the time to prepare a strategy to overcome the enemy that may well attack in the future. How can we be best prepared to overcome in the battle of the mind?

Transformed not conformed

A vital aspect of the Christian life is that we should be committed to God in both body and mind. In Romans 12:1-2, Paul says

> Therefore, I urge you brothers, in view of God's mercy, to offer your bodies as living sacrifices, holy and pleasing to God – this is your spiritual act of worship. Do not conform any longer to the pattern of this world, but be transformed by the renewing of your mind.

The renewing of our minds seems to be a foundational part of our relationship with God. That renewal flows from our commitment to him, expressed in both physical and psychological ways. The mind is the site of decisive battles in our lives. If Satan can dominate our thoughts, by adding loads of false guilt or wrong teaching, then there is little chance that our bodies will be living sacrifices to God. Most of the skirmishes that we lose on the field of the body we probably lose in the mind first. The record of King David's sin with Bathsheba is that he lost a battle of lust after seeing her bathing in her back yard. Only then did he go on to summons her and from that big mistake he ended up in adultery and arranging for her husband's death. In the film *Fatal Attraction* the character played by Michael Douglas has an affair that leads to terrible consequences for his wife and child, as well as death. His one night stand seemed so innocent to him at the time but he came to regret its consequences deeply. It all began with a brief conversation at a bar during a party. You can almost see the battle going on in his mind. Decisions made in the heat of desire have an enormous impact. The war was lost in the mind, even though the action took place in the flesh.

The pattern of this world is constantly before us. The media bombards us with a value system that is totally foreign to Christian ideas. All around us people are living life to a set of principles that are contrary to the mind of Christ. This is why it is so important for us to choose the renewing of our minds if we want to fight illness on all fronts. Sometimes the pattern of this world is shocking. Chris, for instance, was unfaithful to his wife on their wedding day! His act of betrayal was so gross that it was even featured on a BBC2 documentary called *Betrayal*. He and Sarah had lived together for four years when they decided to get married. They splashed out £10,000 on the event and stood in front of a Christian minister in a church building making vows of faithfulness to each other before God.

At the start of the reception, the bridegroom spilt something on his jacket and made the excuse that he wanted to change his clothes. He went home with the wife of the best man and committed adultery with her. Four weeks later he left his new wife and set up home with the woman who had been the wife of his best friend! Both Chris and his lover appeared before the television cameras to explain their reasoning.

'If you want something badly enough' Chris said, 'then you have got to go out and get it and if someone else gets hurt in the process, well, that's too bad.'

'Yes', added Debbie, his lover, 'my view is that life is too short to put off having whatever you want. I wanted Chris and he wanted me and that's all that matters.'

In a society where many people share such beliefs, we need transformed minds if we are going to live in a way that pleases God and does no harm to others. Contemporary wisdom says 'Please yourself': Jesus said to his heavenly Father 'your will, not mine be done.' In the kingdom of God, the way up is down! It's the upside down kingdom where Jesus taught that those who would be great should become the servants of all. In a rat-race society of selfishness and hedonistic indifference to the feelings of others, we need to submit our minds to the renewing power of the Spirit and the Bible.

Eat for victory!

In order to win significant victories in the battle for the mind, we need the right mental diet. When troops go into battle, it is vital that they take the right rations. Failure to do so could lead to vulnerability before the enemy. For the Christian believer, our battle rations are in God's word, the Bible.

Most people seem to think today that if you don't have a daily paper, listen to probably at least three or four radio news round-ups and watch at least one major television news programme per day, you are missing out. Twenty-four hour news is the expected norm – 'the news in fifteen minutes every fifteen minutes, twenty-four hours a day' as Sky News boasts. When we moved to live in the majority world, I went through a kind of media withdrawal! No newspapers, no television and apart from the odd nine minute burst of 'The news from London' on the BBC World Service occasionally, no daily news service. It nearly drove me crazy. What I soon came to realise is that while I had been in Britain, I had been subjected to information overload. Every news story is analysed and inspected and commented upon to a ridiculous extent. We can become depressed by this constant diet of bad news. In such an atmosphere evil thrives and good news doesn't usually get a look in.

The same is true of our regular diet of films, magazines and books. Parents rightly concern themselves with what their children are reading and watching, but what about themselves? Adults can make choices of their own, but do they always do so wisely? Too much of this kind of material can undermine our Christian values and cause problems for us as we try to combat suffering and pain. Escape it may be and that has its place, but we need to be aware that we will be affected by what we watch, read and hear. This is why the apostle Paul wrote Philippians 4:8–9

> Finally, brothers, whatever is true, whatever is noble, whatever is right, whatever is pure, whatever is lovely,

whatever is admirable-if anything is excellent or praise-worthy – think about such things . . . And the God of peace will be with you.

Christians should be informed about what's going on in the world, but we need to beware of information over-load and the danger of filling our minds with an unhealthy diet. Tabloid attitudes make poor rations for a soldier of Christ on active service. If we want to have victory in the battle for the mind, then we had better pay attention to our food intake. John Stott was right when he suggested that Christians should pray with the news-paper in one hand and their Bible in the other.

The Power of Positive Claptrap?

I do not believe that positive thinking is the key to over-coming in the mind. Several years ago a well-meaning friend gave me a copy of Norman Vincent Peale's book on the power of positive thinking and there have been many imitations since. Now while there can be no mis-taking the benefits of a good outlook on life and no doubt about the health-giving effects of a cheery optimism, it is simply not enough to guarantee survival in the appalling struggle with chronic pain or disability. The renewing of the mind in Christ is much more than this.

- It is about letting Jesus in to the dark areas of our past. He only comes in by invitation, as in Holman Hunt's painting of Christ as the Light of the World, the artist has painted no handle on the outside of the door that represents our hearts. He only comes in where he is invited to come and be Lord, offering his light to shine into our darkest secrets with forgiveness and grace.

The handle is only on the inside and we must use it by faith to open the door of our lives to him.

- It is about letting the Holy Spirit take up residence in us so as to produce the fruit of his presence, love, joy, peace, patience, kindness, goodness, faithfulness, gentleness and self-control (Gal. 5:22). When people pray for us, they create a channel for God to fill us with the Holy Spirit and when we pray too, a highway for God is opened up.

- It is also about making a conscious decision not to fill our minds with horrible stuff that gets us down. There is enough distress and suffering around us without us creating more for ourselves unnecessarily. We need to choose each day to fill our thoughts with wholesome and grateful things, so that God can get a look in. That's not clap-trap, that's plain common sense.

Getting our focus right

Whilst working as missionaries in Zimbabwe, Diane and I found that we could only take on board so much of the suffering around us and had to learn when to switch off. At times we felt guilty about this, because the needs were immense, but we would have been of no use to anyone if we had gone under ourselves. I am not saying that we were hard or unfeeling, but we focused on what we could do and tried not to think too deeply about what we could not achieve. The only exception to this was in planning and prayer where we tried to look beyond our own boundaries to see what God was doing and what more we could do in response to the suffering around us. This is what Jesus did. He was not driven by the immense needs around him; he was led by what he saw the Father doing.

This altered focus must be a lifestyle for us at all times, but especially in adversity. If I had a broken leg and it was in plaster, I would not be able to carry other people's bags for them. It would only be temporary. The day would come when the cast was removed and my pain was over. Then I would carry their burdens as I should. Till then, I would pray for them and encourage them with my words and example, but I simply could not do what should not be done physically. I have had to remember this lesson in these years of extreme pain. I know that there are terrible things going on in the world, but right now I am fighting my own battle with agony and need to know where the boundaries are drawn. I have also chosen to edit my intake of entertainment carefully too so as not to undo the good that God's word and his promises are achieving in my heart. There is enough real horror in my life without the added weight of fictional horror.

Every Christian should be fully engaged in the real world. Believers are not called to live in a Christian bubble where everything is perfect and peaceful. Jesus did not and neither should we. But there are times in our battle for the mind when we need to regroup and plan our strategy to overcome adversity. That planning will involve reviewing our media intake and regularly assessing our sources of information. If troops fighting in the battlefield knew that their enemy had access to the kitchens where their rations were made, they would intensely scrutinise their catering. That is what we need to do and for the same reason.

Chapter 2

Asking the Right Questions

We nicknamed her 'the Tiger.' She was the senior surgical resident on the team that had operated on me at the Middlesex Hospital in London in August 2005. She earned her moniker on the very first day that we met her. I had arrived on the ward after yet another long and gruelling journey with my wife from our home island of Guernsey. I had not even had time for a cup of tea and a biscuit before reporting to the ward where I was met by this female doctor. Nobody had warned me what to expect on this admission and I had come prepared for a two or three day stay. In fact, I would not go home for two and a half weeks. Nor was I prepared for what would come next.

'Take your clothes off right now and get ready for a drip to be fitted in advance of us putting in a Hickman line' (a kind of intravenous artificial feeding device that I had known before when spending time in Intensive Care – not a pleasant experience).

'What for?'

'You are going on six weeks of total pancreatic rest before your surgery. You have eaten your last meal. You won't even be able to drink water from now on.'

It almost seemed as if 'the Tiger' was enjoying herself. She relished telling me that I would hate this regime and that it would probably keep me in hospital for the whole time. Thankfully, a kinder doctor came around some time later and reversed the decision to put in the Hickman line, opting instead for a tube which would enable me to go home in a couple of weeks once I had mastered it. Not a morsel of food or a drop of drink (not even water) would pass my lips for the next six weeks.

Several weeks later, I had undergone major abdominal surgery and was waiting behind the curtains for the doctors to do their rounds. Sadly, I could tell from the shrill tones emanating from behind my neighbour's curtains that 'the Tiger' was in charge that day and was in good voice. She swept into my cubicle, followed closely by an entourage of frightened minions. To my horror, she declared that she was going to 'take down' the sealed dressings that covered my huge wound and proceeded to take up the corner of my sterile bandage with her long fingernails. I was appalled. There were several cases of the hospital-acquired infection MRSA on my ward and I knew that she had not had time to wash her hands between the next bed and my own. Her impetuosity was literally putting my life at risk. I took a deep breath.

'Excuse me, Doctor,' I said, holding her hand by the wrist, 'but have you washed your hands?'

She blanched and stared straight at me. I could feel the shockwave reverberating around the group of medical students, before whom she was evidently showing off. Some of them averted their eyes and looked intently at their notes. Others suppressed a giggle behind their hands.

'Well actually, no,' stuttered the now reddening Tiger, 'I haven't, but I did use an alcohol rub between patients. Will that do?'

'No, I'm afraid it won't. As you know there are several cases of MRSA on this ward and I would be grateful if you would go and wash your hands first.'

'Ah. I don't think we need to take this dressing down at the moment' was her reply. 'We'll leave that to the nurses later.'

With that, the Tiger spun on her heels and was gone and I had learnt an important lesson. It is good to ask the right questions!

Questions of God

Despite their fear of God, good people in the Bible threw some hefty questions at the Lord. They were not shy, nor afraid of saying things that might worry others of a less robust faith. They poured out their queries and issues before the Lord. Sometimes they got answers and sometimes they did not but, in each case, the asking of the question was a righteous and necessary part of their ability to endure. It is also important to ask the right questions both of health providers and of those who minister in the area of divine healing. We need to look out for integrity, transparency, genuine compassion and a sound theology of suffering, as well as a theology of healing. When we see these things we can proceed with confidence. When they are absent we should beware. As Rob Bell says in his controversial but refreshing book *Velvet Elvis*: 'Questions, no matter how shocking or blasphemous or arrogant or ignorant or raw, are rooted in humility. A humility that understands that I am not God. And there is more to know.'[3]

But why are we so poor at asking straightforward questions – of our doctors, our Christian leaders, even of God himself? Is it that we don't want to hear the answers? Or do we feel that it is not our place to do so? Perhaps we feel that it is impertinent to ask questions, especially of the Almighty? Yet questions are frequently found in the Bible, especially in the Psalms, as something worthy, right and healthy in themselves. While Job's friends were portrayed in a bad light for questioning Job's integrity and the scribes and Pharisees were condemned for trying to trip Jesus up with their questioning, other questions were permitted or commended.

In Genesis 18, another man not afraid to ask questions was Abraham, who engaged in a question and answer session with God or his representatives, from which the Lord did not withdraw. In fact, the discussion between Abraham and the God of all the earth that follows the revelation of God's plans for the overthrow of Sodom gives the appearance of a robust argument. Abraham asks increasingly daring questions about the point at which God would be prepared to step in and preserve the lives of the righteous and God accedes to his demands. If Abraham's attitude was wrong, then surely the Lord would have told him or silenced him. In a similar way, again and again in the book of Psalms, writers ask searching questions of God.

> How long, O LORD? Will you forget me for ever? How long will you hide your face from me? How long must I wrestle with my thoughts and every day have sorrow in my heart? How long will my enemy triumph over me? Look on me and answer, O LORD my God. Give light to my eyes, or I will sleep in death (Ps. 13:1–3).

The ability to ask questions is part of the divine image in us, put there as a result of God's creative work. We bear the image of the Creator in a way that is unique amongst God's handiwork. Like speech, walking on the moon and crying tears, the asking of questions is a sign of our elevation above the animal kingdom. Human beings have always asked questions like 'What would happen if I tried this?' or 'Why can't we do that?' and the results are obvious. The history of our inventiveness and development as a species is built on our gift for asking searching questions. It's a God thing.

Rob Bell suggests that the art of questioning God is also central to our Christian experience. He warns against belligerent, arrogant questions that have no respect for our Maker, but commends honest, vulnerable questions that arise from the awe involved in engaging with the living God.[4] In the beatitudes, Jesus declared as blessed those who 'hunger and thirst after righteousness'. That is not the same as hungering and thirsting after knowledge or information: rather a real desire to do what is right before God. But it does mean that Christians are supposed to be 'hungry and thirsty' for something beyond themselves. It is this that leads to asking questions about what is going on and what God is doing in our lives.

The Prince of Darkness

I was sitting in the comfortable but old-fashioned farmhouse kitchen of a Christian doctor. He was a friend but also a professional involved in preparing missionaries for overseas service and debriefing them on their return. I had been to see him several times during our time abroad. Now I was visiting him because I was struggling with the aftermath of my first time in Intensive Care. I realised later that I was suffering from post-traumatic stress due to the horrors that I had been through. What left me with a real dilemma were the terrifying nightmares and paranoid delusions I had known as a result of the toxins in my system, combining with a lack of oxygen and the effects of the medical form of heroin. I had been literally having bad trips.

For most of the time I was in the ICU I had been convinced that the nurses were trying to kill me. I fantasised that they were stealing drugs from the locked opiates cabinet and selling them on the streets. My tortured mind convinced me that they thought I would inform on them and so they were determined to silence me. I believed that gunmen were lying in wait for my family when they visited me and on one occasion I thought that they had put my bed outside the hospital on the grass – I could even feel the rain falling on my face! I saw demons and horrifying apparitions and became convinced that one of the cleaning ladies was a witch who had cursed me. I was so terrified once that I soiled myself in fear and had to be held down by security staff to stop me pulling out tubes and wires, while the nurses sedated me.

Months later, in the comforting quietness of my doctor friend's home, as I listened to the rhythmic ticking of the old clock, I asked 'Can you help me answer one question? I had been a Christian for thirty years prior to my first encounter with acute haemorrhaging pancreatitis and have always loved the Bible. I avoid horror movies and any violence on television and I refuse to read anything too graphic or bloodthirsty. I am basically a gentle guy and a caring pastor so where did all that horrible darkness and evil come from?'

Even the act of asking the question made me shudder as a cold wave of shame and fright curled down my back and broke over my lower spine.

'In Matthew 13:27 there is a very pertinent question asked by the servants of a landowner who was experiencing real problems with weeds in and among his crop.

"Sir, didn't you sow good seed in your field? Where then did the weeds come from?" they asked. "An enemy did this," he replied. Although most of what you are describing is common to patients in Intensive Care, especially when they are full of opiates and toxins and have a high fever and low oxygen levels, there is another dimension.'

'You mean the devil got in on the act?'

'Yes. This must not be over-stated or exaggerated but there is a personal, malevolent force at work in God's world that will take any opportunity to oppress God's children.'

'He certainly oppressed me. But doesn't that make me guilty in some way?'

'Not if you believe that Jesus was sinless in his life as the Messiah, because, describing him in prophecy, Isaiah said "He was oppressed." So you were in good company.'

And then I remembered a Bible verse that Diane felt she had been given by God when I was at my worst in ICU and there was likelihood, medically speaking, that I would not pull through. She heard God speaking to her through the words of Jesus to Simon Peter: 'Simon, Simon, Satan has asked to sift you as wheat. But I have prayed for you, Simon, that your faith may not fail. And when you have turned back, strengthen your brothers' (Lk. 22:31–32). When I was conscious and calm enough for her to share this with me, Diane said that she felt that there had been a real spiritual battle going on for my life and sanity. She was also encouraged by the implication that when I had recovered, my task would be to strengthen others going through the same sort of circumstances. I told my doctor friend about this.

'She was right', he said 'and what's more, the prayers of your friends, and of Jesus himself, would have been a vital element in overcoming Satan's attack at that time.'

'So my question was not silly then?'

'What do you mean?'

'I feel stupid not understanding that basic fact of spiritual warfare, but when you are in it, sometimes it is hard to focus on these deeper issues. It's certainly impossible to pray for yourself.'

'That's when you need praying friends you can rely on.'

Thank God we had them and still do.

But over the years of this struggle there have been other questions I have asked. These are some of them and I know that they are common. I hope that sharing them will help others who are asking them right now.

'Why me?'

One of the most frequent questions I have asked the Lord during my long battle with serious ill-health is 'Why has all this happened to me?' Like the disciples sitting at the table during the Last Supper who asked the Lord 'Is it I?' when told that one of them would betray him, I felt that I must have done something terrible to have suffered so much and for so long. Whenever I had a procedure done by the medical or surgical teams, designed to help me, they invariably made me worse. Side effects and failures which were normally only expected in a tiny minority of patients, perhaps one or two per cent at the most, would turn up in my case. Despite being soaked in prayer during operations from which others walked away virtually unscathed, I would find myself being faced with all kinds of complications.

Neither did I find it helpful when some clever people suggested that instead of asking the question 'Why me?' Christians should ask 'Why not me?' as there are no sound reasons for thinking that believers in Christ should be any different to anyone else. Hasn't God promised to protect his people? Doesn't it say 'If you make the Most High your dwelling – even the LORD, who is my refuge – then no harm will befall you, no disaster will come near your tent. For he will command his angels concerning you to guard you in all your ways' (Ps. 91:9–11)?

So my question is worth asking. The answers that I have received to it over the years have come from various sources, some that I did not expect. Firstly, they came from medical practitioners. There was a Christian doctor that I met not long after my first skirmish with near fatal acute haemorrhaging pancreatitis. She was glad that I was doing well enough, after several months, to go out. But her question floored me: 'What do you think Jesus has been saying to you in all this?'

This winded me. I had not paused during my conflict to even consider the possibility that God might be saying anything at all to me in this struggle with a deadly disease. I stammered through my reply and got away as quickly as I could. When I got home, I settled down to pray and ask this important question: 'Lord, what have you been trying to say to me through all that has happened during the last few months?' That turned out to be a very important moment for me and one that came under the general heading of 'Why me?' It was also one that affected me deeply for some time to come.

The answers that I got over the next few weeks were personal, but were a great encouragement to me. I am sharing some of them with you only to give you the incentive to do your own asking. My answers may not necessarily be yours, but they may give you some pointers. I started, for instance, to spend time thinking about the first couple of chapters in the book of Job in the Old Testament. There I found insight into why Job was plunged into the most awful suffering, in which he lost health, wealth, family and personal reputation.

All this happened to him, firstly, not because he was being punished for some terrible wrongdoing, but rather because God was proud of him and his faith. 'Have you considered my servant Job?' the Almighty enquired of the devil. Secondly, although Job suffered the physical, mental and social consequences of enormous pain and loss, the real reason for it all was going on behind the scenes in a spiritual realm. The apostle Paul seemed to have some kind of similar thinking about his own difficulties when he claimed that his own imprisonment, for instance, was working out for the furtherance of the gospel, when to all intents and purposes it might have seemed that the very opposite was taking place. Thirdly, I saw that Job's trials were time limited and that there came a day when God said 'That's enough' and they were over, and that gave me hope for the same outcome in my own circumstances.

One interesting point regarding our questions arises from the book of Job, in that when God answered Job's questions, he did so by asking him questions. The last couple of chapters of Job are built on God's questioning of Job and his friends: 'Where were you when I laid the foundations of the earth?' The fact that God did that has a double effect for us. Firstly it establishes the fact that God's eternal kingdom is full of questions and is infinite – so that means it is always going to be one step beyond our ability to comprehend it. Secondly, it serves as a warning that though our questions are legitimate and acceptable, they simply may not gain for us the answers we would like. They may simply serve to raise even deeper questions – but that's not a bad thing. We must approach our interrogation of the Almighty from a position of humility, always standing ready to embrace mystery and acknowledge that only God knows. This position of faith and surrender requires from us a relationship with God in which we know that he is good and we choose to trust him, even if we don't fully understand him or his ways. That's a tough call, but it is what biblical Christianity offers us as a foundation for surviving the storm force winds that life throws against us.

When you know and love someone, your relationship with them can carry through some deep misunderstandings. I shall never forget when I announced to Diane one day that God was telling us (notice the plural – I didn't!) that we were to leave our pleasant and fruitful ministry on the south coast of England and venture north to get involved in church planting on the outskirts of Manchester.

It was a disaster from the moment we started. Our car broke down on the motorway and when we arrived at the car-park behind the church, somebody crashed into it as we walked away from it. In those days I only owned one suit and we put it into the dry cleaners. The shop burned down overnight, my jacket and trousers with it. We stayed in a single room behind the screen of an Asian cinema – you can imagine how noisy our nights were. It was the so-called 'winter of discontent' with bakers' strikes, firemen's strikes and rubbish piled high in the streets. And worst of all, Diane knew in her heart that I had made a huge mistake but I would not ask for her opinion!

Her amazing love for me carried her through that low point in our lives. The relationship survived (just) the immense pressure I put upon it. That's how it is with God. When we have a relationship with him and feel his love, we know that we can trust him even if it seems as though everything is going wrong. We know that he is good and only wants to do for us what will be eventually for good (Rom. 8:28) even though there are times when we simply cannot see how. By the way, we left Rochdale three months later and I had learned some huge lessons.

We live in a fallen world

Along with my consideration of what the Bible says, God answered my 'Why me?' question in other ways. Consultants and specialists explained to me why my body was behaving in this terrible way. In all this, there was a growing acceptance in me that we live in a still fallen world. Sin and sickness continue to be part of the common experience of man. Even as Christians who understand the spiritual dimension of what is going on, we need to be practical and focus on the reality of all that is happening in our fallen bodies. For this reason, it is good to ask and to understand what is being done and why. I find that the medics are more willing to explain things than they used to be, although some are better at doing so than others.

Not all my questions have been directed at God or other people. Some of them I ask of myself. Such questions are also important in the process of getting through storm force winds and surviving. There was another question I asked myself many times over – and you may do so too.

Is there a scrapheap and am I on it?

The fireman stood near to the entrance of the church. All around him, bits of broken car were raining from the sky while, in the background, dull explosions thumped the air, causing him to wince and me to duck.

'We have got to evacuate the building' he yelled above the shouting firemen and the warble of sirens from tenders about to join the fray.

I had a hunch this day would come. We had built the new church at Delancey in Guernsey on prime sea-front land, but in front of a car-breaking yard where a huge and growing pile of vehicle carcasses towered over the church spire. It was only a matter of time before one of the bright sparks who worked on the yard gang used a blowtorch or match to illuminate the inside of a petrol tank to see if it was empty – and 'kerboom' – up it would go and perhaps the church with it.

I had watched that scrapheap daily as I went to my office at the church. Following that particular fire, the worst of many, the authorities closed it down and the huge mound of broken cars slowly disappeared. It seemed so sad to me that there should be such a heap of uselessness in a place of stunning natural beauty. I also thought that some of those wrecks were good enough to go on for a while. Having lived and worked in Zimbabwe, I know that there most of them would still have been going, some of them as taxis. It's all a matter of attitude and regulations, but there could be life in the old wrecks yet.

Since I became so ill, I have often reflected on Bernie's yard, as it was called, and wondered if its proximity to a busy Pentecostal church was a comment on how we Christians treat people who hit hard times. I have wondered if people with chronic conditions and intractable

problems are pushed to the margins and overlooked in
the bid to make the church successful. Is that how God
treats them? 'Is there a scrapheap in God's kingdom and
am I on it?' is my frequent question. Over the years of
chronic ill health I have come to the conclusion that the
answer is no – but only just!

How do I know there are no scrapheaps in God's
economy? One dictionary definition of the word is 'a
place to discard waste material'. When it comes to people with whom God is in relationship through Christ, he
simply doesn't have any waste material to discard. In
the Bible, God tells me that he has made a covenant with
me and that I belong to him forever. Ever since the book
of Genesis, God has been in the business of making
covenants with people, in which he undertakes respon-
sibilities as their Lord and Protector and calls them into
relationship with himself. And that's the essence of this
argument. There can be no scrapheaps where there is
true relationship between God and his servants. That
relationship and love matter so much more than what
we can physically do or not do, as the case may be. An
ownership document for a vehicle only holds good for
as long as the vehicle serves its original purpose and
gets put to one side when it is time to scrap the car. But
a covenant – that's a different matter. God's covenant
with Noah was for his day and beyond: 'I now establish
my covenant with you and with your descendants after
you' (Gen. 9:9). The covenant that God made with
Abram was called 'an everlasting covenant': 'I will
establish my covenant as an everlasting covenant
between me and you and your descendants after you for
the generations to come, to be your God and the God of
your descendants after you' (Gen. 17:7).

As people of faith in Christ, we are children of
Abraham (as he later became). And didn't Jesus talk

about covenants? 'In the same way, after supper he took the cup, saying, "This cup is the new covenant in my blood; do this, whenever you drink it, in remembrance of me"' (1 Cor. 11:25). So God's offer of a relationship with us is for a period far beyond our useful span of service, and is not dependent on our ability to perform.

When I was spending a lot of time in hospital a few years ago, I became very concerned about my uselessness. The church that I was supposed to be serving was holding some special services and Chris Bowater, the well-known songwriter and worship leader, was the invited guest. He found out that the pastor who had invited him was in hospital and came to visit me.

I was embarrassed to see him because I felt so hopeless, being holed up in hospital while leading a major Pentecostal church with a healing ministry! In his attitude towards me he showed me the real heart of God. He came into my room and hugged me, with his warm tears falling onto my pillow behind my head. He told me that if I could never do another work of service, my heavenly Father would still love me and enjoy having fellowship with me, his child. I don't like the phrase, but I was gob-smacked! In the midst of one of my biggest scrapheap experiences, this kind servant of God assured me that even if I couldn't perform any more acts of Christian ministry, I was not finished yet as far as God and his covenant were concerned.

And there, I suppose, is the ultimate answer to my question. How can there be a scrapheap in a kingdom that has no end? 'And his servants shall serve him' is not written for this world alone. In fact, whatever happens to us down here as Christians is but a pale shadow in the light of what will be our experience of God and his covenant-keeping faithfulness in eternity. God enjoys our fellowship way beyond any return that we might bring to him or his kingdom.

According to an Old Testament expert, the Hebrew word for God's covenant-keeping faithfulness is *chesed*. It means that his kindness towards us in covenant relationship is neither temporary nor based upon our own ability to perform. Norman Snaith writes '*chesed* has to do with mercy and forgiveness, but its true significance, as the *chesed* of God, is that it is everlasting, determined, unshakable. Wonderful as is His love for His covenant people, His steady persistence in it is more wonderful still.'[5]

The people of Israel were often unfaithful to God and treated his *chesed* with contempt. As a result, they went through periods of terrible exile and banishment from his felt presence. But they were not utterly cast off forever and God still has a place and a plan for Israel, despite all her failings: 'If we are faithless, he will remain faithful, for he cannot disown himself' (2 Tim. 2:13).

There is no scrapheap in God's kingdom and I am not on it. And neither are you, despite your pain and frustration. God has only started with us and he most certainly is not yet finished. Though we can only guess at what he might be up to, the eternal faithful God that we serve has plans for us, plans that will not be abandoned no matter how big the pile of scrap grows or how high the flames rage.

'For I know the plans I have for you,' declares the Lord, 'plans to prosper you and not to harm you, plans to give you hope and a future. Then you will call upon me and come and pray to me and I will listen to you.

You will seek me and find me when you seek me with all your heart.

I will be found by you,' declares the Lord, 'and will bring you back from captivity. I will gather you from all the nations and places where I have banished you,'

declares the LORD, 'and will bring you back to the place
from which I carried you into exile' (Jer. 29:11–14).

God's refinement heap

A friend of mine called Barbara is a remarkable lady. She
has brought amazing comfort to so many through her
work firstly as a care nurse and more recently as a
Christian counsellor. When she heard the idea that I felt
that I might be on the scrapheap, she said 'God doesn't
have a scrapheap, only a refinement heap!' That helped me
because it reminded me that God does not waste any of our
experiences, good or bad, and that he is constantly at work
changing us into the people he wants us to be. At the heart
of this activity is what we are rather than what we do. God
is more concerned with my character than my achieve-
ments. Refinement is a recurring theme in the Bible. From
the book of Job to the epistles of the New Testament, we are
told that God works like a refiner of precious metals. He
heats up our circumstances so that the dross can be
removed and the resulting metal is made as pure as can be
(Job 28:1; Mal. 3:2–3; 1 Pet. 1:7). The process is never easy
but God's purpose is clear. He wants to use the finished
item in a different setting where its beauty will shine for his
glory. Refinement is painful, but it is also preparation for
future usefulness and glory. That idea goes some of the
way in answering my next question.

'What's the point of all this pain?'

This particular question (which I still ask daily!) has no
final answer, but I have received some helpful insights
from God over the years that have enabled me to hang

in there, despite the pain. It illustrates another way that my questions were answered and this is even more sub-jective and difficult to explain. I felt that God spoke to me, in the quietness of my own heart, at times when I was in greatest need. I know you might think it was the morphine speaking and once or twice it certainly was, but enough of good and God's ways came through to convince me that the Lord himself had spoken. I am not talking about hearing an audible voice, at least not in my case, though it has been known. Rather I had the impression that God had spoken. What he said to me was both shocking and at the same time strangely com-forting.

A franchise in pain?

I felt that God said that he had trusted me with this trial because he knew that, with his help, I would come through it and still keep on believing in him. There are shades of Bible truth here. Isaiah was called by God to go for him into his contemporary world with a message that was going to cause him personal pain. Tradition has it that he died as a martyr in the most distressing cir-cumstances, possibly as one of those faithful people who were sawn in half, according to Hebrews 11:37. Ezekiel was called to lose his much-loved wife by sudden death so that he could be a sign to the rebellious nation of Israel (Ezek. 24:15–27). Paul went through terrible adversity in pursuit of God's calling in his life (2 Cor. 11:22–28).

None of that, and especially not my own pain, comes anywhere near what Jesus suffered on our behalf. Without wanting to attribute virtue to pain in a masochistic way, I wonder if Jesus now offers his followers a kind of franchise? Maybe in our own relatively small trials we represent him in some way and there is a sign value to what we go through? Then our trust becomes much more than hanging in there. It is a display of God's grace and mercy in holding us up. As franchisees – not of pain but of God's grace – we become a source of hope for others.

Once I began to think about this, I could see that God was teaching other people, particularly in my family and in the church that I served as pastor, to persevere in prayer and not to give up over the long haul. They were also being caused to ask themselves questions about their own trust in God and his ability to help and sustain them in adversity.

A fellowship of his suffering

I also felt that God spoke to me about the fact that in some way I was entering into the sufferings that Jesus himself went through on the cross. This was shocking for me, but it became practically meaningful at a time of intense crisis. The guy in the next hospital bed to me was waiting for the same major operation on his pancreas. He was a drug addict and his partner would shoot him up with his drugs, illegally, behind the curtain from time to time. We were both operated upon by the same surgeon on the same day and were given both a general anaesthetic together with an epidural one – by injection into the cavity around the spinal cord. This latter procedure was done to ease the post-operative pain that can be so awful after this kind of surgery. In my case the epidural failed and I experienced the most appalling agony, almost beyond my ability to endure. My addict neighbour experienced wonderful relief because of his epidural and was soon sitting up in bed cheerily entertaining the ward while I was rolling and screaming in distress.

The only sense that I can make out of that is that a couple of days later, when I finally did get some relief and spent time during the night praying and asking God my question, the only insight I was given was that on the cross Jesus was offered a typical anaesthetic of that day (vinegar mixed with gall) but had to refuse it. One of the reasons that he did so was in order to endure all the pain inflicted on him by the need to carry away our sin. I am not presuming any kind of vicarious suffering for myself, but I did feel for a short time the significance of the verse that says we are called to share in 'the fellowship of his sufferings' – 'I want to know Christ and the power of his resurrection and the fellowship of sharing in his sufferings, becoming like him in his death' (Phil. 3:10). At least I felt that Jesus understood how I felt and had been there before me and that gave me a degree of comfort. I even sensed that he was saying to me 'I've been there. I know how that feels.' As for the unfairness of it all – that is something to which we shall return later in this book. For now, it is enough for me that when I asked God the big questions, I did start receiving answers, even if they came from unexpected quarters and were not the answers I would have liked to receive. So keep on asking those questions.

Chapter 3

Dealing With Anger

A doctor nearly killed me. He had a reputation for being good at gastro-enterology, but he must have been absent during that part of his training when they covered the subject of bedside manner, he was so arrogant. I did not find it easy being treated by him, right from the start. He did warn me that, with the impending procedure there was a danger of death, but he did so in such an offhand manner, saying 'I have never killed anyone yet, ha ha' that he left me with little choice but to go through with it. In the event, despite warning signs that he chose to ignore, the result was a long and terrifying stay for me in the Intensive Care Unit, some near-death experiences and over a decade of incredible pain.

As you might imagine – sticking with my Christian tendency for understatement – my wife and I have felt angry towards this gentleman. She was angry because of her protective care for me and I was mad because of the threat that he posed to my life and the consequent damage done to my ministry. I did not see the doctor concerned again, because very wisely his colleagues decided that he should play no part in the fight for my survival and others took over. But there were several occasions when he walked past Diane during my stay in

the ICU. True to form, he kept up his arrogant noncha-
lance and ignored her. She raged with fury every time
she saw him and despite her natural sweetness and
calm, told me later that if she had not been confined to a
wheelchair at the time with sciatica, she would have at
least hit him, if not killed him.

Anger has played a very real part in my battle to overcome long term illness and pain. Sometimes the anger has
been helpful in giving me the determination to survive.
Most of the time I have struggled with my feelings and
thought that as a Christian and especially as a pastor and
Christian leader, I should not feel this way. Anger may be a
perfectly natural response to unfairness and perceived
injustice, but is it right for a Christian to be angry? Aren't
Christians supposed to be always calm and polite?
Didn't the Bible even say that we should never be angry?
Isn't anger one of the seven deadly sins? Certainly my own
anger has reared its head many times throughout the period of my struggle and it has been exacerbated occasionally
by the attitude of others, especially Christians, towards me.

I had never found anger to be helpful in the course of
my ministry up until this point. On those few occasions
that my professional calm had slipped and I had 'lost
my cool' I had not noticed any benefits. In fact, the opposite was the case and I usually made situations worse by
my attitude. This, combined with my experience as a
sufferer of long-term serious illness, has driven me to
make a special study of anger and its effects on our battle to overcome, and I have come to some conclusions.

It's normal!

Anger is perfectly normal and a part of our humanity,
made in the image of God. Like other aspects of our

make-up, it was grossly distorted and damaged by the fall of mankind into sin at the very start of time, but it is still part of God's creative work in us. This means that there is an element of our anger that God looked on after he had created man and said was good, and then there is a dark side that needs to be redeemed and brought under the reign of Christ in our hearts. Like sex, which God invented and declared to be good, the devil has hijacked anger and turned it into a mainly destructive force. Everybody gets angry at some time or another. It is a perfectly normal part of our nature. What makes that anger healthy or unhealthy is what it does to us: is it our servant or our master?

God gets angry

Those who know their Bibles know that God gets angry too. When Moses had cold feet about doing the thing that God was asking him to do and suggested that somebody else might do it, 'Then the LORD's anger burned against Moses . . .' (Ex. 4:14). Later, when Moses did obey God and the nation of Israel was called out of slavery in Egypt and on towards Canaan, they baulked at entering the land at Kadesh Barnea. Then 'the LORD's anger burned against Israel and he made them wander in the desert for forty years' (Num. 32:13). Much later still, around the time of the Babylonian exile, Jeremiah explained that 'It was because of the LORD's anger that all this happened to Jerusalem and Judah and in the end he thrust them from his presence' (Jer. 52:3). All these Scriptures and many more like them show us that the God in whose image we are created is capable of many emotions and among them is anger.

But these statements in the Hebrew Bible are tempered by others that reveal that in the heart of God, this anger is under strict limits. Indeed, the anger of God is set out as part of his loving nature – a righteous response to the mistreatment of his people or their refusal to enter into the beneficial relationship he offers them

> The LORD is compassionate and gracious,
> slow to anger, abounding in love.
> He will not always accuse,
> nor will he harbour his anger forever;
> he does not treat us as our sins deserve
> or repay us according to our iniquities
> (Ps. 103:8–10).

> But you, O Lord, are a compassionate and gracious God,
> slow to anger, abounding in love and faithfulness
> (Ps. 86:15).

If God, who is good, gets angry, then anger in itself is not sin and is not off limits for the Christian. This ability to feel and to express anger is also seen in the life and ministry of Jesus. John's gospel records the events in the Temple courts

> In the temple courts he found men selling cattle, sheep and doves and others sitting at tables exchanging money. So he made a whip out of cords and drove all from the temple area, both sheep and cattle; he scattered the coins of the money-changers and overturned their tables. To those who sold doves he said, 'Get these out of here! How dare you turn my Father's house into a market!' His disciples remembered that it is written: 'Zeal for your house will consume me' (Jn. 2:14–17).

The energy in this passage can be keenly felt, as it must have been by its first century witnesses. There would have been a sharp intake of breath from onlookers and nervous cries from their frightened children. The visiting rabbi hurled himself at the marketplace traders in the courts of the temple with a frenzy that must have been exceptionally intimidating. His whip of cords was no idle threat. Tables were overturned and coins scattered everywhere, clattering over the stone floor. Sheep and cattle were crying out and running around wildly in order to escape. Doves flapped their wings in a frenzy, constrained by their wicker cages. Women screamed. The only comment made by his bemused disciples was that they recognised that his zeal for his Father's house was all-consuming. Jesus was angry. Yet, Jesus did not sin. He lived his life in sinless obedience to the commands of God and was in his own nature a picture of what God is like (Heb. 4:15).

How does this story make us feel? If we have been brought up to believe that all anger is bad, then we will probably feel uncomfortable with it. Some have found this passage so difficult to square with their understanding of what Jesus was like that they have ignored it altogether. Others have tried to downplay it, perhaps because it doesn't fit with their preconception that all anger is bad. But however you look at it, Jesus was angry about the injustice going on in the temple, a place designed for prayer, and he did something about it that was clear, forthright and forceful. Yet he did not sin. We need to learn how to deal with our natural anger and to express it in clear, forthright or even at times forceful ways, yet not to breach the boundaries that protect us from doing that which would be sinful or harm others.

Letting ourselves down

We can become angry when we fall below the standards we have set for ourselves. Most of us have high self-expectations, hopes and standards that we have developed over the years since our childhood. Our mistakes and shortcomings become a threat to the picture that we have in our minds of what an all-together adult Christian ought to be. We may attempt to overcome our anger by blaming others or our circumstances but if we are honest, we know that we are angry with ourselves.

When serious illness comes, we can feel particularly vulnerable and unable to do anything about it. I felt angry with myself for not being able to carry on as the senior pastor of a large city-centre church when I first got ill. I berated myself for not doing my duty as I perceived it and was angered by my own weakness and symptoms. That anger was perfectly understandable but it was neither a healthy thing for me nor an aid to recovery. I needed to understand the threats that were facing me – threats to my credibility, reputation and to my future financial security – and deal with the anger in a healthy way.

Angry with God?

Most significantly for a practising Christian, we may become angry at God. We feel that somehow God has let us down. We remember certain promises made in the Bible to protect us from evil and wonder why a God of love would allow things to turn out as they have. For me, there was a theological issue here. I held firmly to a theology of healing which believes that God has

revealed himself in Christ as a compassionate and healing God. My continued illness, despite the amount of
prayer that I received, seemed to fly in the face of that
understanding. I knew some Christians who disputed
the fact that God heals today, but I could not see it that
way. It would have been easier to go along with them
and let go of my hope of healing but there were practical as well as biblical reasons why I could not do that.
The fact that God heals some begs the question as to
why he does not heal all who ask. It also put me in the
strange position of believing in a healing God and praying for others, while I remained seriously and chronically ill. To be honest, this made me mad. I was angry
with God and I know that my wife and son were too and
so were a number of people who were praying for me. Is
it ever right to be angry with God?

If we take the Bible as our guide, then there are signs
that it is acceptable for us to be angry with God and that
we should learn to express it in healthy ways. I will
come back to this in a later chapter, but the Scriptures are
very honest about recording the angry cry of God's servants in the face of circumstances that they could not
understand and found difficult to accept. In one particularly poignant passage, a part of the Bible with which I
can identify very closely, Jeremiah argues that he has
always served the Lord and does not understand the
way that things have worked out for him

> You understand, O LORD;
> remember me and care for me.
> Avenge me on my persecutors.
> You are long-suffering – do not take me away;
> think of how I suffer reproach for your sake.
> When your words came, I ate them;
> they were my joy and my heart's delight,

for I bear your name,
O LORD God Almighty.
I never sat in the company of revellers,
never made merry with them;
I sat alone because your hand was on me
 and you had filled me with indignation.
Why is my pain unending
 and my wound grievous and incurable?
Will you be to me like a deceptive brook,
like a spring that fails? (Jer. 15:15–18)

Again, later in the prophecy, Jeremiah makes direct allegations against God

O LORD, you deceived me and I was deceived;
you overpowered me and prevailed.
I am ridiculed all day long;
everyone mocks me (Jer. 20:7).

What can we do about it?

We need to recognise that there is a dark side to anger. Jesus warned about allowing anger to lead to hatred in Matthew 5:22. Paul said 'In your anger do not sin: do not let the sun go down while you are still angry' (Eph. 4:26). So an early stage in dealing with our anger is to ask God to cleanse us from any unrighteousness. Only then can we go on to deal with the expression of normal anger in healthy ways.

In coping with my anger I have found real help in praying it out. The lesson of God's word is that when we do feel angry with God, we need to tell him about it. He is big enough and loves us sufficiently to be able to bear the weight of our anger and we need to pour it out before him. Sometimes when we pray we feel that we should use decorous language, suitable for the Almighty to listen to. But he knows us so well and cares for us so much, that he would prefer that we cry out and express our true feelings before him: 'Cast all your anxiety upon him because he cares for you' (1 Pet. 5:7).

We also need to find ways of telling others who care about us how we feel. In doing so, we need to find those who, by training or experience, hopefully both, will be able to hear our problems and know enough to help us without being damaged by them.

There was a pastor whose wife died. Some time later he was asked by a counsellor how much anger he had and he replied that he had none at all. When the counsellor probed his feelings in the aftermath of his bereavement, the pastor admitted that he was 'hurt' by the loss of his wife but felt no anger. When the counsellor asked how he felt generally when people expressed their anger, he said that he did not appreciate it. Apparently he did not believe that Christians should ever express anger. When faced with the possibility that he might be denying his anger and even suppressing it, the pastor confessed that this was the case. Afterwards he wrote

> Since I have acknowledged my emotions and have allowed myself to accept how I feel, I am enjoying so many good feelings of joy. After they explained things to me, I came to see that when I stuffed my bad feelings down I also did the same with my good ones. It's so freeing to be myself and experience the joy of walking in who I am in Christ – that I can have normal emotions, like Jesus did when He lived upon the earth.[6]

Another healthy response is to recognise that anger can serve us in good ways. Just as pain is not always bad but can give us as a warning that something is wrong with our bodies, so anger can be a useful servant. It can galvanise us into action. Sometimes when I am angry, I get that deep down sense of 'Right then. Let's deal with this' or 'I'll show them!'

Anger is usually caused by two major things, either a threat to us or our well-being in some form, or a response to injustice. The threat mechanism is very strong and is fundamental to what we are as human beings. This idea is developed further by Andrew Lester in his excellent book on the subject.[7] We become angry whenever we identify a threat, whether it is to our physical well-being, our financial future, our self-esteem or self-worth, our values and principles, or to those whom we love and care for. When we sense that threat our adrenalin surges and our 'fight or flight' mechanism cuts in. That protective mechanism had enabled Diane to be an excellent advocate for me during long periods of unconsciousness or extreme pain in hospital. I have heard her raging at the nurses' station for more morphine or for a doctor to be found, driven by her righteous anger aroused by my need.

The other major cause of anger is a response to injustice. William Booth was angry when he saw the plight of the child prostitutes on the streets of London and devoted his life to doing something about it. William Wilberforce was enraged by those who profited from the proceeds of the slave trade and did everything within his power to bring it to an end. On a more personal level, we feel angry when we see people that we love suffering dreadfully with no good reason for it. When bureaucracy makes stupid mistakes or takes advantage of those unable to stand up for themselves, our anger rises and often gives us energy to protest. This kind of righteous anger, indignation, is close to the anger expressed by Jesus at the temple. It is the kind of anger that Diane felt when she saw the result of the doctor's carelessness and negligence in my case. It is the good side of anger, but still needs to be expressed in healthy ways that do not threaten our (or anybody else's) well-being.

Writing letters can be one way of expressing indignation about how we or our loved ones have been treated. I still have Diane's hand-written protest to the authorities at the Southampton General Hospital after a particularly nasty experience I had in their Intensive Care Unit. The letter was passionate, honest and clear – but still makes me shake in my shoes to read it! The reply she got was indifferent, but did at least acknowledge her grievance and promised to look into it. The very act of writing the letter lanced something in Diane's anger and enabled her to cope with a very distressing situation. Others set up campaign groups, or write web logs (blogs), or get in touch with their MP, or do whatever it takes to express how they feel in productive and meaningful ways.

In my case, I have also written letters to God. I write them in my journals – my everyday record of how things are in my spiritual life – and occasionally in actual letter form. I tell him how I feel and what I would like him to do about it. I set out my distress in writing so that I can see clearly what the issues are. The paper gets fairly hot from time to time. If these epistles are in my journals, then they survive for me to reread them in the future. In letter format I have been known to set fire to them as a way of sending them to God and saying 'Here you are then – what do you say about that?' It may sound daft but it helps me.

Steps for handling our anger with God

There are some things that we can do when we realise that we are angry with God. They are not easy, especially if we are in chronic pain. Like Jeremiah, we need to find a place where we can deal with our anger instead of letting it dominate us.

- We need to be honest with ourselves and admit that we are angry and that the cause of that anger is how we feel God has dealt with us. The process of owning our anger with God will be an important one for us, as we are so often prone to dismiss it as unimportant or to deny it as being unworthy of a Christian.
- Then, in the same way as with anger in general, we need to pour it out before the Lord in some way. If this cannot be done alone, we should seek out the help of a trusted Christian friend or pastoral counsellor to share how we feel. If you are anything like me, I prefer the solitude of open spaces to do business with God and often walk the cliffs or the beaches and address him in loud terms! I only hope that the wind takes my voice away from other people, although these days with mobile phones, nobody seems particularly bothered if someone is walking along having a passionate conversation with an invisible person.
- We need to acknowledge the mysteries that there are in God's kingdom. Basically this is an acceptance that we don't have all the answers, only God does. There always will be mystery in our relationship with the Lord because he lives in eternity while we are limited to time alone and cannot see beyond our immediate circumstances.
- After that we must make a conscious decision to choose to believe that God's ways are higher than ours (not just different to ours) as it says in Isaiah 55:8–9, and that he knows what he is doing. Like it or not, Romans 8:28 is in our Bibles and the fact is that in all things God is working for the eternal good of those

who trust in him and are called to follow his purposes.

- Following this, we need to renounce our right to have all our questions answered this side of heaven. We have the right to ask – but some answers will only be known in eternity. There is a major difference between believers in the West and those in the developing world where I have served as a missionary. In such places they suffer greatly for their faith, as also in life in general. Christians are not immune to this. Their children die of preventable diseases. Their lives are blighted by poverty, just like those of the non-Christians around them. Yet although this is a generalisation, on the whole their attitude is one of powerful acceptance of their lot in life and they have confidence in the love of a good God. Their Christianity is joyful and persistent, irrespective of the mysteries of life and death. Maybe it is because of different standards of education, but there is a willingness to let God be God and to accept that we cannot comprehend all his ways. In the West we expect answers in life as a whole. But if God is infinite, almighty, all-powerful and all-knowing, there is no way that my puny brain can take in all that he knows and does. Acceptance of that fact will be a big step towards dealing with our anger. We will look again at the whole issue of mystery in the Christian life later in this book.
- Finally there is the matter of choosing to trust God – which involves forgiveness for our perceived hurts – even when we cannot understand his ways. I was preaching at a church in north eastern Poland recently and the issue of forgiveness came up. I had been talking to the congregation and the leaders about 'persevering in trials' and confessed to them how angry I have been with God and with others. They understood

because they have suffered so much as a nation. They were oppressed by the Russians, then the Nazis and then the communists again, and have been the victims of so much poverty, persecution and violence over the centuries. Nowadays the folk in this Pentecostal church face hardship because of opposition from Roman Catholic authorities and employers. When I began to speak about forgiveness as a key to letting go of anger, they were transfixed. They began to see that forgiveness must extend widely and even include our willingness to let go of our resentment against God. This is an important issue for people in pain.

In the aftermath of taking some of the steps I have outlined in this chapter, it would be good to express your forgiveness towards God and yourself, as well as to others, in prayer. These words may be helpful to use, either on your own or with someone else.

> I choose to forgive you Lord, for what has happened in my life, knowing that I cannot understand why you allowed it to be so. I forgive myself too, on the basis of what Jesus did for me on the cross, confident that you accept me in Christ washed clean and made new. And I forgive (here you might want to put in an appropriate name/s) for their part in all this and release them to you, for you to work in their hearts in the way that only you know how to do. Thank you for being there for me through all this, even though I have been so angry with you. Help me to rest in your love and release these feelings to you whenever they return. In Jesus' name. Amen

Chapter 4

Handling Our Guilt

Welcome to Guiltsville. A lot of people live here permanently and some, like me, visit regularly. The town has a down-trodden look with neglected public areas and once beautiful gardens that are now past their best. Despite the numbers of people here, very few folk speak to each other and those that do mainly talk about themselves and their own particular network of problems. You get the feeling that nobody is listening. All around the town are signs saying 'Private: Keep Out!' and 'Trespassers will be Prosecuted.'

There are a lot of churches in Guiltsville. Most of them are well attended and the clergy are kept busy. The one that I attend has a congregation mainly made up of clergy anyway, who tend to frequent services on Mondays because they are too busy elsewhere on the Sabbath. We look a dejected bunch, with big black bags under our eyes and a haunted expression about the brow. We all carry elaborate diaries and organisers and, if we are not careful, mobile phones that bleat continuously. It can be hard to get us to switch them off but there are frustrated ministers' wives in the vestibule begging us to do so and in some cases the pleading works.

I think I probably visit Guiltsville at least weekly and sometimes more frequently. I feel the need to go there whenever I think that I have let anyone down. This is especially the case when I imagine that I have let God down, which is even more often – most of the time really. I have a theory that people who are ill long-term are more regular visitors to Guiltsville anyway, because of their tendency to imagine it must be their own fault that things are as they are. If they are Christians and particularly if they believe in the God of the Bible and know that he is a God of healing then, like me, they probably assume they are simply getting their just desserts.

That's what Steve thought. This is how he put it in an article in *Christianity* magazine. He is a journalist who spent most of his first twenty years or so arguing that there was no God and trying to discourage those who said there was. Then he attended an Alpha course with the girl he loved and realised his mistake. Having become a Christian, Steve and his young lady, by then his wife, faced the devastating news that their unborn child was almost certain to die. They received prayer and wonderfully, their child was miraculously healed in the womb. Great!

Some years later, however, they came across the same kind of problem when another child was desperately ill with diabetes and coeliac disease. This time prayer was less successful and Steve and his wife became very discouraged. 'Many times we have felt like second-class Christians,' said Steve, 'punished by God because of a lack of faith.'[8] It seems that no amount of previously answered prayer and things going well can keep you out of Guiltsville when you start down the road that says 'This is all down to me and my faith.'

The teaching of the New Testament is that God heals in response to prayer because of his amazing grace and

compassion and not because we deserve it or can produce anything that he would want in exchange for it –
not even faith. Steve and his wife were no more or less
guilty in either of their crisis situations, but God's purposes for them at each stage in their family's life were
different. It is perfectly understandable, though, that
Steve felt as he did because he was mixing with people
who kept telling him that the result of his praying was
all down to him and not God.

Apparently, according to these recruiters for the estate
agencies in Guiltsville, you can box God into a corner
with certain prayers by saying things like 'I am already
healed' or 'It was all done two thousand years ago and
now all I have to do is believe' and God will automatically be legally bound to do whatever you tell him to do.
When he isn't, and he doesn't, the only alternative is a
quick trip to Guiltsville because you have obviously let
the Almighty down in some way. This matter is dealt
with on a more reflective and theological level later in
this book, but for now it is enough to say that we have
to rethink our understanding of God and his ways in
this matter if we want to get out of Guiltsville – and stay
out.

A wonky conscience

The whole issue of guilt is a complex one in the Christian
life. We need a certain amount of guilt to keep us aware of
what is right and wrong. It can also serve the Christian as a
way of knowing how God feels in some circumstances. We
have within us a conscience which can learn what is good
and acceptable to God. This conscience becomes refined
through the various experiences of life, together with our
developing understanding of God as revealed in the Bible.

Sadly, however, sometimes our consciences can be damaged. They can be badly affected by experiences in our early childhood so that our understanding of God is shaped by what we have known in our key relationships, more than by what we read about him in the Scriptures. A damaged or faulty conscience can be a real problem for a Christian and may lead to false guilt which stands in the way of spiritual and mental wholeness. We will return to this important subject when we look at the issue of perfectionism. Until then, we need to recognize that our consciences may not always be the good guide that we think they should be. Rather like satellite navigation systems that are not always as accurate as they are meant to be, our consciences can lead us astray.

A guide to guilt

Guilt is basic to much human suffering. No other subject occupies the time spent by pastors and counsellors in talking with those who seek their help as much as guilt. Whether speaking with those affected by depression, addictions, loneliness, grief, marriage and sexual problems, enduring sexual or physical abuse, guilt is always a factor and compounds both diagnosis and cure. Sometimes guilt is objective – the result of bad choices and sinful actions taken by the person concerned. In such cases, guilt is appropriate and needs to be dealt with by applying the solution available in the gospel. Appropriate guilt might follow any breaking of the law, betrayal of the trust of others, especially those whom we love, or offence against our own deeply held standards of morality. It causes feelings which are proportionate to the seriousness of the offence caused. Such guilt needs to be brought to the Lord, knowing that in Christ and through his work on the cross, there is a full and perfect solution to appropriate guilt. It is called 'cleansing' and 'forgiveness' to use the language of faith.

Other times, however, the guilt people feel is subjective. This is inappropriate guilt which produces feelings that are way out of proportion to the seriousness of an act, or may even be present when no actual wrongdoing has taken place at all. This is most clearly seen in what has become known as 'victim's guilt' in the case of those abused as children, who believe that they must have done something terribly wrong themselves, either in the act of abuse or what led up to it. Victim's guilt can lead to self hatred and even, in some cases, self harm.

There is also 'survivor's guilt' which can happen when people pull through the most appalling circumstances and others don't. Those who survive often feel an enormous amount of inappropriate guilt that they survived instead of others. They have no objective reason to feel guilty but those feelings are real, and can be aggravated by unhelpful comments made by the relatives of other victims or the media. It isn't just survivors who can find other people's comments increase their feelings of guilt: it can happen to any churchgoer.

Sadly sometimes well-intentioned parents, teachers and preachers make it difficult for those who struggle with inappropriate guilt as their comments, lectures and sermons are often designed to induce guilt in the listener. This may occasionally be done for the best reasons – to bring about change or growth. Or it can be done for the lowest of motives such as inducing higher levels of financial giving. There is a place for teaching and preaching that allows the Holy Spirit to convict of sin and leads the hearer to penitence and change. But that is different from the pulpit-thumping browbeating that sometimes passes for preaching and leaves a trail of guilty, broken people behind.

Though I may have inadvertently done this myself in the past, I now try hard to avoid it. When I have described my struggles with chronic ill-health and its many effects in my life, people have often said that it was such a change to hear preaching that did not condemn or make sufferers feel inadequate or guilty. A young mother said that she had just got back from a Christian conference week where she had been made to feel such a failure that she despaired of ever being worthy to even attend church again. She had found it so helpful to hear that God has dealt with our guilt through Christ and that there is 'now no condemnation for those who are in Christ Jesus' (Rom. 8:1).

The long shadow of shame

One aspect of subjective guilt that affected me during my long-term illness and pain was the intense shame that I felt for needing such strong medication. On the ward in a London teaching hospital I was in desperate pain. I needed another shot of morphine, but did not ask for it because the nurse who was in charge of me had revealed to me that she was a Christian, originally from the Philippines. She went to a large Pentecostal church nearby whose pastor I knew well. I felt so guilty that I was also 'a man of God' in her eyes and yet needed powerful opiates to survive. Then a wonderfully wise and godly Free Church hospital chaplain explained to me that my shame and guilt were inappropriate. She felt that I ought to give thanks for the medical advances that have made such discoveries possible and receive the drugs with gratitude. When I did so, I was able to overcome my embarrassment and ask for relief. If we can receive the food that God has provided with a prayer of thanksgiving, even though it may be synthetic or man made, why can't we 'say grace' and accept painkillers and antibiotics as his gifts with thankful hearts too?

Very often, both before and since that episode, I have come across Christian sufferers who struggle with guilt at needing regular medication, never more so than when such treatment is for anxiety or depression. Yet, with those drugs, just as with insulin and morphine, people have discovered the healing properties of these naturally occurring and synthetic substances in order to help their fellow human beings. The original creating work was God's and he deserves our thanks.

Objective guilt – the real thing

The Scriptures deal with the issue of objective guilt – our legal position before a holy God defined by our sin. That sin is precisely the reason why Jesus came into the world and gave his life on the cross. There is now the possibility of a marvellous exchange – my sin for Christ's righteousness. Romans 3:24–25 puts it like this

> God did it for us. Out of sheer generosity he put us in right standing with himself. A pure gift. He got us out of the mess we're in and restored us to where he always wanted us to be. And he did it by means of Jesus Christ. God sacrificed Jesus on the altar of the world to clear that world of sin. Having faith in him sets us in the clear. God decided on this course of action in full view of the public—to set the world in the clear with himself through the sacrifice of Jesus, finally taking care of the sins he had so patiently endured (*The Message*).

Once we know that this full and complete work of forgiveness and reinstatement was done for us – an actual event in space and time – then we have no grounds to hold on to our objective guilt any longer. We have been set totally free of all our wrongdoing by the work of Christ and placed in a position of acceptance with God and his people (Eph. 1:6–7). The record of our wrongdoing has been erased – the slate washed clean. In Psalm 103:12 it says that 'as far as the east is from the west, so far has he [God] removed our transgressions from us'. In the mind of the person who wrote that Psalm under the inspiration of the Holy Spirit, the east and the west were not places but directions! Because of what Jesus did on the cross, our sins are going in one direction and we are headed in the opposite way. This means that we and our sins are not scheduled to meet again, not even at the judgement day. They are gone and we need to learn to live free of them and their effects.

The phrase 'no condemnation' in Romans 8:1 must mean what it says or it would not have been put there for us to read in the first place. Apparently God does not expect people who believe in Christ to live in Guiltsville. He wants them rather to live lives free from condemnation, in grace and acceptance by him. Instead of trying to produce enough good works to appease an angry deity, we rest in his kind invitation to follow Christ and leave Guiltsville behind. As for me, I have visited the place enough times to realise that I do not want to stay there permanently. If I can choose each day to remember how much my heavenly Father loves me and what he has done on my behalf in Christ, instead of focusing on my sense of failure or regret, there is no need for me to ever go there again. Let's see how long I last!

Chapter 5

Issues of the Heart

1. Control

I am a passenger on an Aurigny Trislander aircraft flying between the islands of Guernsey and Jersey. These bright yellow planes are well known to us in the Channel Islands but are usually a source of amusement to tourists, who arrive at the local airports having never seen one before.

Fourteen passengers are sitting two by two in line astern of the single pilot, side by side and looking over his shoulder. The noise and vibrations of the engines are fearsome, reminding me of being in a washing machine at full tilt. Suddenly the aircraft lurches violently and the pilot doubles up at the controls. He has collapsed and the plane is now without its captain.

'Don't worry!' I yell from my seat half-way down the fuselage, between the two wing-mounted engines (the third one is up on the tail above the passengers' heads). 'I'll save us.'

At that, I launch myself forwards over the shoulders of the screaming travellers in front of me and claw my way to the seat beside the stricken pilot. I haul myself in beside him and grab the earphones with the attached microphone from his head.

'Mayday, Mayday' I cry, in a reasonable imperson-
ation of the famous Tony Hancock sketch. 'This is Eric
Gaudion flying a Trislander south of Guernsey and the
pilot has just collapsed. I have only ever flown gliders
before but with your help I will land this plane and save
all on board.'

It is at this point that I invariably wake up trembling.
That dream must be the most frequent one I have, apart
from the one where I am speaking at Spring Harvest and
turn up on the platform wearing only my underwear. I
don't need to spend a lot of money on counselling to
interpret this nightmare because I think that I have got a
good idea what is going on in my head. I may be suffering from what might be described as control freakery
and even occasionally suffer from the delusions of a
messianic complex. Where did all that come from?

Ever since my childhood, I have had a very strongly
developed sense of responsibility. My brother has learning difficulties and so from an early age I was put in
charge of him while my Mum was busy helping my Dad
in the family business. Wherever I went, I usually had
my brother in tow and so I grew up quickly, with a sense
that I was responsible for somebody else's well-being
and I was in control. This misconception was shared by
others who saw in me a mature and sensible individual
who could be given even more responsibility. So I was
appointed as a leader at school, in the scouts and cadets
and at Bible College: in fact, wherever I went. It also led
to a lack of the simple irresponsible playfulness and
carefree fun that should be part of every childhood. I
suppose I could be forgiven for forgetting who is in
charge of my life. I have had to return again to this issue
in my battle with illness. It is a matter that we need
to get settled if we are going to fight illness on all
fronts.

A control freak?

We probably all know the uncomfortable feeling of being dictated to by a card carrying control freak. I know one who cannot help raising his voice to drown out anyone else's opinion in a discussion. The volume and tone get higher and higher until every challenge to his superior knowledge is silenced. Perhaps you have worked for a boss whose harsh and demanding regime is an expression of their desire to rule every aspect of your life if you will let them? No matter how interesting or convincing your ideas may be, they always insist on doing things their way, even if it turns out to be more expensive or less effective. Of course, an element of control freakery is part of natural assertiveness and the need to be able to influence your surroundings and be noticed. When I told Diane that I was going to write a section on being a control freak, she immediately quipped that this was going to be an autobiography. Even our tiny Pomeranian dog has got a very strong will and, if we let her, will control every walk that we take. What leads to this normal expression of self-assertion going over the top and becoming unhealthy?

The fear of being vulnerable

The first reason for it is the awful discovery of our own vulnerability. This can happen in the maturing process as we grow up. A published expert on control freakery, Les Parrott, has explained that 'as we mature, we realise we're far less powerful and far more vulnerable than we had ever imagined. So we sometimes cling to the illusion, trying desperately to put back the pieces by once again cultivating over-controlling tendencies.'[9]

This sense of vulnerability often returns when we are chronically ill or in pain. We become keenly aware of our own weakness and sometimes, in order to compensate, can become over-controlling. This leads to a lack of trust in health professionals and people who care for us and can make their job a lot more difficult, as well as being lonely and counter-productive for us. Allied to this feeling of vulnerability is our perennial enemy, fear. Fear can dethrone the sense of God's sovereignty in our lives and cause us to stew in a mess of emotions, even having physical consequences. According to the Bible, fear and perfect love cannot cohabit. As we grow in our sense of being loved by God and by others, we can gradually repent of our fear and put ourselves in God's loving hands. But, as I have discovered, that is not an easy thing to do. It would take a crisis to teach me that doing so was the only sensible step to take.

Who is in charge?

During a long time in which I was confined to bed at home as part of my recovery from the first attack of acute haemorrhagic pancreatitis, there was a hand-written card at the bottom of my bed, stuck to a wardrobe. 'God's in charge around here' it proclaimed, 'not me, not the doctors, nor my illness. Romans 8:28.'

Diane had written it and put it up and it remained true even if I didn't feel like it all the time, and it certainly caused a few raised eyebrows among the doctors and district nurses who visited me. There was at least one occasion when my breathing stopped and I was so critically ill in that room that an ambulance was called to transfer me back to hospital. I can still remember the comfort Diane's sign gave me as I was wheeled past it, gagging for oxygen and survival.

With my background and attitude, the matter of control is significant and had to be addressed as part of my recovery. In Colossians 1:15–20, Paul is concerned that 'in everything he [Jesus] might have the supremacy.' But is that true for us? Here's how the apostle put it

> He [Jesus] is the image of the invisible God, the firstborn over all creation.
>
> For by him all things were created: things in heaven and on earth, visible and invisible, whether thrones or powers or rulers or authorities; all things were created by him and for him. He is before all things and in him all things hold together. And he is the head of the body, the church; he is the beginning and the firstborn from among the dead, so that in everything he might have the supremacy. For God was pleased to have all his fullness dwell in him, and through him to reconcile to himself all things, whether things on earth or things in heaven, by making peace through his blood, shed on the cross.

This is possibly the text of an early Christian hymn or praise song. Singing it helped the Christians of that day to remember whose side they were on in the battle to keep believing despite their suffering. It sets out in a memorable way the antidote to some false teaching that was being put about amongst the believers at Colossae concerning who Jesus was. Some said he was a good man, a religious leader or teacher but not God, much as some still do today. The passage comes in two parts: the first (vs15–17) shows us Christ's supremacy in creation and the second (vs18–20) Christ's headship in the Church and in the act of redemption. When we are suffering, or someone dear to us is, we sometimes make the mistake of imagining that the devil is in charge, calling all the shots in our circumstances. Verses 16–17 teach us otherwise.

When we compare them with the amazing list in Romans 8:38–39 of the full extent of God's love towards us in Christ, then we see that there are no limits to how far the creative power of Christ and the love of God in Christ extend: 'For I am convinced that neither death nor life, neither angels nor demons, neither the present nor the future, nor any powers, neither height nor depth, nor anything else in all creation, will be able to separate us from the love of God that is in Christ Jesus our Lord.'

Think about the challenge of that passage in Colossians. Is Christ reigning as Lord in your heart? Or are you struggling to keep control? Have you come to a place where you can say that 'in everything he might have the supremacy'? Why not pray the prayer of Paul also from Colossians 1? If we change it to the first person, it will say something like this (in a paraphrase of *The Message*):

Dear God, I pray that you will give me a wise mind and spirit attuned to your will, so that I may acquire a thorough understanding of the ways in which God works.

I pray that I'll live well for you, my Master, making you proud of me as I work hard in your orchard. As I learn more and more how you work, Lord, I will learn how to do my work. I pray that I'll have the strength to stick it out over the long haul – not the grim strength of gritting my teeth but the glory-strength you give. It is strength that endures the unendurable and spills over into joy, thanking you, the Father, who makes us strong enough to take part in everything bright and beautiful that you have for us.

God, you have rescued us from dead-end alleys and dark dungeons. You have set us up in the kingdom of the Son you love so much, the Son who got us out of the pit we were in, got rid of the sins we were doomed to keep repeating. Amen.

2. Identity

The phlebotomist had just arrived on the ward and was looking for me in order to take blood (that's what phlebotomists do). She trundled her trolley over to my bedside and gazed at her notes.

'Ah, Eric Gaudion' she said. 'I have to get a bit of blood from you today as there are several tests to be run on it.' At that she took hold of my wrist, straining to check the armband that the nurses had put on me.

'Wait a minute,' she said 'you're not Eric Gaudion. You're John Denham.'[10]

'No I'm not. I may be a bit woozy on all this morphine but I do know who I am.'

'Someone's given you the wrong name tag then – and I'll bet John Denham won't be too pleased to find that out either.'

Later, the shame-faced staff nurse who had admitted me came to tell me the whole story. John Denham was a poor old chap who had been flown in from Alderney, one of the other Channel Islands, in a state of confusion. Apparently he was given the name tag that I should have been wearing and then escaped from the ward. He was knocked over at a traffic roundabout not far away and brought back by ambulance into the Accident and Emergency department, unconscious. There he was identified from his name tag – as me!

Thankfully, they had not yet got round to notifying his (my) family of his now greatly deteriorated condition, or I can just imagine the shock that would have caused. I am also grateful that I was not given any of his medication or, worse still, subjected to any unnecessary surgery as a result of this careless incident. My name tag was sorted out straight away. Thankfully Mr Denham turned out to be not too seriously hurt and was restored to his rightful identity.

In my case, the problem of unclear identity is not one that has been limited to that isolated incident alone. During my long battle with the agony of pancreatitis and its associated admissions to hospital and frequent long and humiliating medical and surgical procedures, I have often struggled to remember who I am. Not that I am referring to my name, although I have known periods of coma and deep unconsciousness when my name tag has been a vital piece of kit. I mean rather the struggle to hold on to who I am during all the processes of care that I endured.

Perhaps you have had difficulty in remembering your real identity while passing through the sausage factory of serious medical care, or undergoing the emotional numbness that can follow trauma or serious ill health. You may have lost your job or your ability to keep your place in some social circle or professional group. Part of your identity, like mine, may also have been tied up in what you hoped to achieve in the future, and all that may have changed radically. If so, as I discovered, there are things that can be done that help.

I found it helpful, for instance, to establish little routines centred around my clothing. In order to counter the dehumanising effect of the system, each time I went into hospital I tried to keep getting dressed in my own clothes in the mornings whenever I was well enough to do so. This had the effect of keeping up at least the semblance of normality and avoiding the humbling, depersonalising consequence of being in pyjamas in public or, even worse, hospital gowns, though this was not always possible.

'You going home today then?' the other patients would ask cheerily, seeing me getting dressed.

'No, just trying to stay sane!' would be my reply.

I also found it helpful to try and hang on to my real spiritual identity, come what may.

Who are you?

From a faith perspective it is important for Christians to remind themselves often of who they are in Christ. Our identity is not just what our parents, our education or our training have made us. We have a much higher and more significant identity than that. Knowing who we are in him makes a very real difference to our attitude towards the circumstances through which we are passing. Revelation 1:5–6 offers a wonderful benediction: 'To him who loves us and has freed us from our sins by his blood and has made us to be a kingdom and priests to serve his God and Father – to him be glory and power for ever and ever! Amen.' It says that God loves us and that he has made us into a kingdom and priests to serve him. That means we are not just a number in a hospital, school or anywhere else. We have royal blood in us. We are princes and princesses in the kingdom of heaven. When you accepted Jesus, he accepted you and put a royal robe around your shoulders. You have a throne beside his. You are seated with him in heavenly places (Eph. 2:6).

The New Testament calls Christian believers 'overcomers.' We overcome the adverse situations we are in by our faith. So that makes us special. In addition to all that, we are new creations, free from condemnation, more than conquerors and destined to rule with Christ in eternity. If we spend time reminding ourselves of these great truths, we shall find it easier to hang in there and keep trusting God, no matter where we find ourselves. Corrie Ten Boom was a Christian who, during the Second World War, found herself in a Nazi concentration camp because of her family's work in hiding Jewish refugees from their oppressors. Even in Ravensbrük, though surrounded by the most appalling human tragedy and in great physical and emotional pain, she reminded herself regularly of who she was in Christ. It saw her through. During her time in the camp she lived for four months in the shadow of a crematorium, yet she described that as being liberating because it enabled her to live in touch with the reality of eternity. She described being aware at all times of God's omnipotence and his caring love.[11] She managed to hang on to her sense of identity, despite the most atrocious conditions around her.

'Physician, heal thyself'

From time to time in my illness I have found myself in the company of other patients who are, in fact, doctors. I have met several GPs and on one occasion found myself next to a Professor in the very university teaching hospital where I – and he – were being treated in the same pancreatic unit. I noticed how hard it was for doctors to become patients in the system of which they usually play a leading part. I suppose that, for them, the identity crisis had become even starker. Their role had been reversed and they found themselves recipients of care instead of givers. Perhaps they also know too much about what goes on behind the scenes. If they have allowed their sense of identity to become tied up in the job that they do, then their time as a sufferer is going to be even more painful than it need be.

This issue can affect each of us, no matter what our job. It can be a lot harder to receive care than it is to give it. I know what it feels like to be utterly helpless in a hospital bed while other people clean me up after soiling myself or being violently sick. It makes you feel like a child again, so wretched and useless. At such times it can be most difficult to remember who we are, but in God's heart nothing has changed. We are still the same people that we were before all this happened to us and he still loves us. If we can hold on to that awareness, it will save us a lot of distress.

Just as human beings are so much more than the sum total of their physical parts, so in Christ our identity remains intact whatever may be happening to us in the physical or even emotional realm.

3. Cynicism

Over the years of my battle with adversity I have become increasingly – and sometimes dangerously – cynical. Cynicism comes as the result of too many disappointments, failed expectations, dashed hopes and the frustration caused by chronic pain. It is a hardening of the soul – an expectation of defeat – where it becomes hard to rejoice in others' victories and difficult to feel hope. In such a frame of mind it is hard to rejoice, exercise faith or even pray. Envy and mistrust are never far away. Cynicism, like bitterness, needs to be resisted and, in some circumstances, should be repented of. It is very emotionally tiring and is best avoided as much as possible by those who are suffering enough already.

Cynicism was around in Jesus' day too. This was how Nathanael responded when he heard that Jesus was calling disciples to follow him. 'Nazareth! Can anything good come from there?' he asked (Jn. 1:46). The Jews of that era were a subjugated people who had suffered enough from claims of messiah-ship and the false hopes that usually surrounded them. And those are features of cynicism. It grows like bacteria in an atmosphere of mistrust and disappointment such as is often found in gatherings of needy people, like busy hospital wards and waiting rooms.

I learned early on that the battle against adversity has peaks and troughs. The highs are hopes raised by some new drug therapy, treatment plan or suspected diagnosis. They can also come through the premature expectation that one has been healed in answer to prayer. When these come to nothing, as they so often do, the troughs can be very deep indeed. Hope deferred makes the heart sick (Prov. 13:12).

At times like this cynicism makes me wary of trying anything new. It even causes me to wonder if there is any point in receiving more prayer. I know others have felt the same. Some have decided not to receive any more healing ministry because they could not cope with the serial disappointments. I also know of one lady who received her miraculous healing after making that decision. In her case, she made an exception when she heard God speak to her clearly and tell her that he was going to heal her. She overcame her cynicism in time to receive a wonderful blessing.

I have made a commitment to combat cynicism and keep trusting God and his power to heal. This is not easy but it is based not on how I feel but on who God has revealed himself to be. My choice is not to let the negative and fearful comments of others get to me but rather to keep on believing that God is good and that he has a good plan for my life. I also choose to believe that my circumstances are in his hands rather than being driven by the whims of others, medical professionals or otherwise. Over time I have developed strategies for combating cynicism.

Strategies against cynicism

There are ways that we can guard against cynicism. Firstly, we can try to remind ourselves that we are not the helpless victims of circumstances. If we put our trust in the living God and place our lives into his hands, there is a higher power watching over us and all his intentions towards us are good and pure. He has a plan for our lives and, difficult as it may be to discern it at times, that plan will be fulfilled for our eternal good (Rom. 8:28). Secondly, we can try to fill the gap in our lives that illness, pain or loss has brought by setting out to serve others.

In Channel 4 television documentary[12] a very rich man went under cover, working as a volunteer in a Portsmouth hospital, with the aim of finding some folk whom he could help with large gifts of cash. In doing so, he came across some remarkable people. One lady had suffered with the agony of spondylosis for over eight years, as well as having had a botched hysterectomy that damaged her for life. She was constantly in pain and relied on morphine patches and a walking stick to be able to move about at all. Yet this dear lady went every day as a volunteer into the hospital, to find patients who could not feed themselves, in order to be able to do it for them. Setting the nurses free to do other things, she gave herself lovingly and sacrificially to serve others. Though she did not do it for reward, she was given a substantial gift cheque at the end of the programme and both the rich man and viewers (certainly in our home) were moved to tears at her bravery and selflessness. In her own way, through the pain, she is an example of what George Bernard Shaw called 'the true joy of life: being used up for a purpose recognised by yourself as a mighty one; being a force of nature instead of a selfish little clot of ailments and grievances, complaining that the world will not devote itself to making you happy.'[13]

Thirdly, we can try to believe the best of people until we are proved wrong. There is no room for cynicism in this description of a Christian: 'Always seeking to be blessed, always looking for the best.' Cynics in hospitals and surgeries will sometimes regale us with their low opinions of those treating us, or of the health service generally. There is plenty of material there to be cynical about – but we can choose not to be affected by it. We may well have to 'lift the shield of faith' (Eph. 6:16) to protect ourselves when others are firing their burning arrows of cynicism at us. Praising small acts of kindness where they do take place and exhibiting a grateful attitude can often defuse this kind of atmosphere. It can also keep us on track against the inroads of our own cynicism.

One of the best ways to combat cynicism and negativity generally in our hearts is by focusing our minds on the truth of God's word. Sadly it is in this area that so many mistakes have been made by well-meaning but mistaken sections of the faith healing movement. Expectations have been built on faulty exegesis of Scripture that sound so fine when declaimed from a pulpit but do not survive the light of clear thought and rational interpretation. It is vital to our battle with storm force winds that we hold on to secure and fundamentally true understandings of what God has promised us in his word. In this way we shall be armed with truth. I have been shocked to discover how many Christians have been led astray in this battle for the soul.

Part Two

The Battle For The Soul

Chapter 6

Armed With Truth

Introduction

'What you need to know' preached the evangelist, 'is that your sins and your sicknesses were all taken away two thousand years ago on the cross. All you need to do now is believe and both forgiveness and healing will be yours!'

I was sitting behind this visiting preacher on the platform of the church of which I was the pastor and was, frankly, squirming in my seat because I disagreed so strongly with him. As he was my invited guest I was not sure how to proceed. I decided to let him carry on without interruption but I stood up at the end to address the congregation. 'As the editor of a famous magazine once wrote, the views contained in this edition are not necessarily those of the editor!'

The people knew me well and understood my teaching on the subject of divine healing, so they also got my drift that Sunday morning and there were some knowing looks in the gathering. Long before pancreatitis, I felt very strongly that healing is a ministry of the Holy Spirit given to us by the grace of God and that while there is an important place for faith in healing, it is not the kind of faith that tries to force God into a corner. Nor do I accept the claim that there is a legal obligation for God to heal us, because of the cross.

In saying this, I have no desire to be negative about the healing ministry in any way at all. The New Testament promises healing through the gifts of the Holy Spirit (1 Cor. 12) and the ministry of elders in the church (James 5:14). Both of these means of grace have been part of my own work and experience and remain so to this day. I have known remarkable touches of divine healing in my own body from time to time. In the mid 1980s, I felt called to full-time radio ministry overseas, but was hindered by persistent allergenic rhinitis. Following a test to discover which allergens were responsible, it was found that I was sensitive to twenty two out of the twenty four test items. Nevertheless, after receiving prayer from the leaders of our church, I was completely healed and able to take up the new ministry.

My back was also healed of a serious degenerative condition of the lower spine in 1994. In 2002 I received prayer at a healing conference in Canada for the problem of pancreatic pain that was, once again, hindering my life and work. As a result of the gracious answer to prayer, I was able to do without pain relief for a whole year – which turned out to be a very significant year in the life of our church. I have also seen many thrilling and miraculous answers to prayer for healing and deliverance in the lives of others for whom I have prayed, even while I myself have been in great pain. This fact is not easy to understand but it is not unusual. One of the founders of the Pentecostal movement in Britain, whose miraculous ministry brought thousands into faith, was so affected by eczema in his hands that he had to lay hands upon the sick with gloves on!

The problem comes when Christians, and preachers in particular, go beyond the scriptural warrant for healing and claim that there is a legal right, purchased on Calvary, for every believer in Christ to be healed from any and every sickness. They also over-emphasise the place of faith, laying great pressure on sufferers to believe sufficiently strongly and blaming them when things don't seem to be happening. It is in response to those two errors that I am writing the next section of this book.

Jesus was a healer and ever since gospel times the Christian Church has been concerned about healing the sick. That concern continues today, never more so than in the hearts and minds of those of us who are chronically ill, but in the last hundred years or so this idea about healing being in the atonement on the same basis as the forgiveness of sins has developed. Until around 1880, it was not part of Christian teaching to any great extent. It developed into the claim, already referred to, that there is a legally binding agreement between God and believers to heal all whose faith is sufficient, in the same way as our sins are forgiven. The few Bible verses that are frequently used, or perhaps misused, in support of this teaching include Isaiah 53:4, Matthew 8:17 and 1 Peter 2:24.

I believe, however, that there are no unambiguous biblical grounds to make those claims. It simply does not make sense within the doctrine of the atonement itself to teach that physical healing and the forgiveness of sin were equal parts of the work of Christ on the cross. Sin and sickness may be related, but they are different. They are not interchangeable. As Dr John Stott says, the one requires atonement, the other does not.[14]

I intend to limit my comments to the issue of whether or not physical healing is ours through the atonement in the same way that forgiveness is. I will not be doing much more than glancing at other forms of 'wholeness' which flow from the work of Christ on the cross. There are undoubtedly many of these. When forgiveness and grace come into a person's life, all manner of ills are removed and prevented. That in itself is not sufficient proof that sin and physical sickness are one and the same thing or that Christ died for them both on the cross. I will present the idea that if physical healing is to be understood as being part of the atonement at all, it may only be so in two limited ways. Firstly, it may be so from an eschatological point of view – relating to the end times – and secondly in an indirect way through the ministry of the Holy Spirit who heals and who only comes to us because of what Jesus did for us at Calvary.

Why bother with this?

There are important reasons for taking the time to consider this subject. Sufferers are placed under enormous pressure by the teaching that forgiveness and healing are at the same level in the atonement. They are led to believe that the entire responsibility for their condition and their problems lies with them. They might also conclude that they remain in their sickness simply because they do not believe enough to be healed. Speaking about this idea, Robert Dickinson comments: 'such a conclusion – one which many boldly and uncompromisingly proclaim – has such terrible and ridiculous implications and brings such torturing doubts and fears into the minds of the unhealed, that it is small wonder that sober-minded men feel the need to think again on the subject.'[15]

It is also possible that sufferers who are taught this idea and remain unhealed will wonder if their sins have been forgiven. This may undermine their assurance of salvation and cause a loss of joy and peace. It also threatens to lessen the impact of the tremendous miracle of redemption achieved by what Jesus did for us on the cross.

Furthermore, churches face the very real danger of schism because of the divisive nature of certain elements of this doctrine and its associated practices. People who believe this teaching sometimes set themselves up as spiritually superior to those who do not, and they act as though they have some kind of inside knowledge – rather like the way Gnostics of the first and second centuries of Christian history behaved. Those who remain unhealed or for whom recovery is a long time coming are regarded as second-rate, particularly in the area of their faith. I still receive letters to this day telling me that my faith must be deficient and that if I only believed more firmly in what Christ did for me on the cross, I would be healed. Sadly there are some people who have struggled to understand their place in the Church because of this teaching and have quietly gone away and been lost to the Christian community altogether.

I am writing to offer some teaching and a theological understanding of the place of healing in the atonement and the part that our faith plays in the issue of receiving healing or otherwise. It is important, both pastorally and practically, that we should do this. I shall look at what this doctrine teaches, how it came about and then examine the relevant Scriptures to see if it is what the Bible says. In doing so I will consider the role that faith plays in receiving healing and also the significance of the phrase in the Lord's Prayer, 'Your kingdom come.' The doctrine of atonement itself needs some explanation if we are to see its benefits clearly.

Chapter 7

The Doctrine Defined

The basis of this teaching that healing is part of the atonement is deceptively simple. Among the Scriptures used to support the teaching is Isaiah 53:5 'by his wounds we are healed'. Kenneth Hagin Jnr comments on the verse: 'It does not say we might be healed, or that we are going to be healed at some time in the future. No, the Bible says we are healed! That's present tense. That means healing is a reality right now. With His stripes we are healed! Healing is a present-tense fact which is already established in God's Word.'[16]

The implications of this idea are then spelt out for us. It is not just the healing ministry that is 'established in God's Word' but each individual's healing. It is, after all, he says, always God's will to heal the sick. It is a sign of unbelief and lack of faith when Christians (especially Christian leaders) pray the words 'Your will be done' with regard to healing. God's will is clear and unequivocal: 'Nothing is left out of the redemptive work of Christ – not a headache, not a stomachache [sic], not any kind of cancer, nor any kind of heart trouble – not any sickness or disease! In God's plan of redemption every sickness and disease has been dealt with!'[17]

This is not just an isolated extract from the tract of an extreme practitioner alone. No, this idea sells a lot of Christian books and is widely accepted. Perhaps one of the reasons why it sells so many books is precisely because it is not matched by people's experiences and so they are driven to buy more books and listen to more sermons in a desperate attempt to understand it more clearly and see it lead to healing in their own lives. David Petts, a Pentecostal pastor and theologian, (who does not go along with the definition he offers here) describes the doctrine thus: '. . . that Christians may claim healing from sickness on the grounds that Christ has already carried that sickness for them just as he has carried their sins.'[18]

Someone who does support this idea, Ray Hubbard, states clearly that just as the punishment for our iniquities fell upon Jesus so that he bore them and 'was crushed on their account', so the 'punishment' of sickness fell upon him in a similar way. This was in order, claims Hubbard, that he might 'make atonement for it' (sickness).[19]

The history of this doctrine

Whilst this teaching has its roots in the healing movement of the early nineteenth century, which itself drew on sources as early as John Wesley, it only became clearly stated in preaching and writing as recently as the end of the nineteenth century. Several fluent speakers and writers of that era, particularly in America, taught and wrote about it around that time, to be followed later by A.B. Simpson. He was the influential founder and first president of the Christian and Missionary Alliance and it was largely through his influence that the teaching spread and was accepted throughout many churches in the USA. The doctrine, which greatly influenced the Holiness movement of the latter part of the last century, became a foundation for the beliefs and practices of the early Pentecostal movement that emerged at the beginning of the twentieth century.

As someone who became a Christian, was baptised and ordained in the Pentecostal church, I can say that it is no longer the universally held position of Pentecostals that Christ's death guarantees restoration to physical and mental wholeness before the final resurrection, though many charismatics and Pentecostals in Britain, the USA and elsewhere around the world do support this view. Certainly the Elim Pentecostal Church in which I was ordained has amended its 'fundamental truths' to remove the earlier statement supporting the doctrine.

One theologian from the Elim position is Dr Keith Warrington who, in his book on healing and suffering, makes it clear that: 'As far as the reference in Isaiah is concerned, it is inappropriate to view this OT prophecy as the basis for an unconditional promise that all believers should be able to claim healing for all their illnesses before they die.'[20]

Other large Pentecostal movements, however, do continue to give strong support for the teaching, more or less as it was originally set out. The largest Pentecostal denomination in America, the Assemblies of God, still declares in its fundamental truths: 'Divine healing is an integral part of the gospel. Deliverance from sickness is provided for all in the atonement and is the privilege of all believers.'[21]

Despite this clear statement, which is set out in even greater detail in a position paper on the matter, debate and disagreement continues. Their position is that although they do believe that Christ made full provision for physical healing in the atonement, our redemption will only be complete at the Second Coming of Christ. 'We receive the forgiveness of sins now in connection with the redemption of our souls. We shall receive the redemption of our bodies when we are caught up to meet the Lord and are changed into His likeness.'[22] This is a healthy balance but not one that receives much publicity.

Alongside the classic Pentecostal movements, representatives of the charismatic wing of the Christian Church have championed this teaching. Colin Urquhart, for instance, once an Anglican priest and now leader of a dynamic faith movement, believes it to be totally inconsistent to say that Jesus died for your sins without also saying that He died for your sicknesses.[23] He goes on to challenge his readers to 'go by what the Word of God says' and believe that Jesus has already done on the cross everything that needs to be done to make the healing theirs. His readers are urged simply to put their faith in that.

Much of the present day emphasis on the teaching comes from the publications and preaching of members of the 'Word of Faith' movement, founded largely by Kenneth Hagin and involving such people today as Morris Cerullo, Benny Hinn and Kenneth Copeland. Hagin himself drew heavily upon the teachings of a proponent of what has been called 'new thought', a kind of pseudo-Christian philosophy set out by one E.W. Kenyon. In a classic work on this relatively recent doctrine, Hagin stated that the original manuscripts leave no room for doubt and that Christ died for our sicknesses as he died for our sins.[24]

There is a lot of controversy around this particular movement. Some evangelical scholars claim that they present a gospel that is foreign to New Testament Christianity. D.R. McConnell famously called it 'a different gospel' in his book by that name.[25] Whatever the rights and wrongs of that argument, a lot of suffering believers have been led to despair by this one particular emphasis regarding healing and we need to think about it more seriously today. If it is true, for instance, then why did the Early Church apostles not preach it? The gospel preachers of the book of Acts did loudly proclaim forgiveness of sins through the cross. If there is an automatic right to healing alongside the forgiveness that flows from the cross, then why did they say nothing about it? What does the Bible teach on this matter?

Looking at Isaiah 53:4–6

In order to resolve this for myself, I set out to understand the biblical teaching as clearly as I could. I did not want to make the mistake of deciding the truth of a doctrine simply on the basis of my own or anybody else's experience. I wanted the Bible to speak for itself, allowing the Scriptures to interpret other Scriptures so as to discover the Bible's own internal evidence. If that is then supported by the evidence of experience then all well and good, but my love for the Bible as the word of God meant that I could not put the cart before the horse. Isaiah said in chapter 53:4–6

> Surely he took up our infirmities
> and carried our sorrows,
>   yet we considered him stricken by God,
>   smitten by him and afflicted.
> But he was pierced for our transgressions,
> he was crushed for our iniquities;

the punishment that brought us peace was upon him
and by his wounds we are healed.
We all, like sheep, have gone astray,
each of us has turned to his own way;
and the Lord has laid on him the iniquity of us all.

This passage is the fourth of the Old Testament Servant
Songs and offers us a glimpse of the suffering as well as
the triumphs that lay ahead of the one who would be
known as the Servant of the Lord. But who is this
Servant? The songs contain obvious references to the
work of the Messiah. If you think about the way that
Matthew and Peter use these verses in the New
Testament, it is clear that in their minds the suffering
Servant refers to Jesus. Certainly the description of the
Servant being wounded and bruised, chastised and
scourged, in order to produce shalom for his people is
enough to make it clear why Christians have tradition-
ally attributed this prophecy to Jesus, and rightly so. So
whilst the suffering Servant songs do have implications
for Israel, they find their complete fulfilment in the one
who was the true son of Israel, the Messiah, Jesus our
Lord.

What will the suffering Servant achieve?

The main theme of the fourth Servant song is the work
of the Servant in redeeming his people from sin. Isaiah
opened the first Servant song against the background of
a peace and a righteousness that had been lost: 'If only
you had paid attention to my commands, your peace
would have been like a river, your righteousness like the
waves of the sea' (Is. 48:18). At the beginning of chapter
49, the Servant of the Lord steps forward to 'bring Jacob

back to him' (Is. 49:5). Where peace was missing, the Servant would restore it through his unique peacemaking work; 'But he was pierced for our transgressions, he was crushed for our iniquities; the punishment that brought us peace was upon him and by his wounds we are healed' (Is. 53:5). The suffering Servant's work would be to bring reconciliation between God and his people and the resulting wholeness and peace into their lives.

Isaiah is using the word 'healed' in verse 5 to speak of healing in a total sense, restoring wholeness and completeness to a person. This wholeness may well have a physical dimension – people may feel better when they give up sinful or harmful practices to follow the Lord – but the context will not allow us to presume that it includes all sickness. The two verses 4 and 5 are the only ones in the Servant song that contain language capable of being understood to include physical sickness as well as sin at all. In fact the original Hebrew words *holi* and *makob* are translated 'griefs' and 'sorrows' in the Authorised Version. The New International Version prefers to use the translation 'infirmities' and 'sorrows'. The Hebrew word *holi* is used elsewhere in the Old Testament in a way that reflects physical illness or disease but, once again, a careful examination of the context here does not support that use of the noun. The way the prophet uses the word in the context of the Isaiah 53 passage means that it should be taken in a non-physical sense here, in a passage that deals heavily with sin and its consequences in our relationship with God. After all, the context is everything in understanding Bible teaching.

The real emphasis of verses 4 and 5 is spelt out in verse 6. 'We all, like sheep, have gone astray, each of us has turned to his own way; and the LORD has laid on him

the iniquity of us all.' These verses are all about our relationship with God and the impact that the work of the
suffering Servant of the Lord will have upon that. Verse
5 talks about 'our transgression . . . iniquities . . . (and)
. . . punishment' all being laid upon the Servant. Clearly
the use of such words in close proximity to the phrase
about being healed requires us to focus on sin and the
form of spiritual dis-ease that it represents. The substitutionary work of the Servant deals primarily with sin.

Another Bible passage that will help us to understand
the meaning of the word 'healed' in Isaiah 53 is found in
Jeremiah 30:12–17. Jeremiah describes the calamity that
has come on the people of Judah – that they have been
carried away into exile in Babylon – as an incurable
wound, an injury beyond healing. Then in verse 17 God
speaks to reassure them that, in bringing their exile to an
end and restoring them to their promised land, he will
restore them to health and heal their wounds. So what is
in view here is the restoration of God's people from the
consequences of their sin and rebellion, which include
estrangement from the promises of God regarding the
security of their homeland and not physical sickness or
ill health. Jeremiah is using the language of sickness fig-
uratively, just as Isaiah did.

In Isaiah 53:6, the Servant's accomplishments are portrayed as the work of the Lord. It is God who took the
initiative and did this, rather like the High Priest in
Israel who once a year took a young goat and confessed
the sins of the people over it, prior to its ritual slaughter
as in Leviticus 16:21 and the Day of Atonement. What
Isaiah has been saying about the Servant's substitutionary role was repeated annually in the ritual practices of
Israel. So the Servant's work is concerned with sin first
of all and then with the effects of sin in the lives of those
who are estranged from God. God presents himself here

in a High Priestly role, overseeing the transference of the sins of the people to the head of his Servant.

Commenting on these verses, a minister with a very real healing ministry, Peter Lawrence, believes that under the old covenant between God and his people, there was a link between sickness and sin. At that time the wrongdoing of Israel did result in some sicknesses being laid upon individuals and sometimes on crowds. This can be seen in the affliction of Gehazi, the servant of Elisha, with leprosy, when he tricked Naaman into paying money for his healing (2 Kgs. 5:20–27). There were also plagues that afflicted the whole nation of Israel from time to time, most notably when David sinned by numbering the people and as a consequence over seventy thousand people died in one day (1 Chron. 21:1–14). All this would account for there being a link in the mind of people then between sin and sickness and lead to a conclusion by some even today that sickness is dealt with in the atoning process. Yet this is no longer the case, Lawrence argues. Under our new covenant relationship with God through the work of Jesus on the cross, we are in a different kind of relationship with God. In this new relationship, our sins are transferred to Jesus. That is where punishment for sin takes place now. He adds 'Jesus Christ did not die for sicknesses; he died for sins.'[26]

A closer look at Matthew 8:16–17

When evening came, many who were demon-possessed were brought to him and he drove out the spirits with a word and healed all the sick. This was to fulfil what was spoken through the prophet Isaiah: 'He took up our infirmities and carried our diseases.'

The words from Isaiah 53:4 are quoted directly in the gospel of Matthew. They come at the conclusion of a remarkable series of healing reports, which included the healing of a leper, of a Roman centurion's servant and of Simon Peter's mother-in-law, culminating in Matthew 8:16 with its reference to the healing of all the sick who were brought to Jesus. The whole passage, which follows the conclusion of the Sermon on the Mount, is intended to provide a demonstration of the power and authority of Jesus. In order to understand this more fully, we need to look at why the gospel was written.

Why did Matthew write?

In the background throughout Matthew's gospel is the relationship between Israel and the Gentiles. This was very much the big issue of Matthew's day. Matthew is fighting a battle between Pharisaic Judaism on one hand and the lack of moral restraint found among the early Greek-style Christian communities on the other. He portrays Jesus as the fulfilment of Old Testament expectations and hopes, applying Old Testament texts to Jesus' life and work. He is offering early Jewish Christians the tools with which to witness to their non-Christian Jewish friends, as well as arguing for the Jewishness of Christ among the Greek converts of the Early Church.[27] Matthew earths the teachings and works of Jesus in Old Testament prophecy, seeking wherever possible to explain what Jesus was doing in terms that devout Jews would understand. For the gospel writer, the works that Jesus was doing in Galilee were a clear fulfilment of Isaiah's prophecy.

'This is what was written'

Matthew makes frequent use of the Old Testament by
means of what might be called his 'formula quotations'
of which there are ten. They begin with variations on the
formula 'This was to fulfil that which was spoken by the
prophet . . .' Chapter 8:17 was one of these formula statements: 'This was to fulfil what was spoken through the
prophet Isaiah: "He took up our infirmities and carried
our diseases."' The meaning of the word 'fulfil' is of special importance to Matthew. He does not use the word
simply as an introduction to a list of Old Testament
proof-texts, but rather as part of his overall presentation
of Jesus as the fulfilment of Old Testament hopes and
therefore Jewish expectations. He uses this phrase as an
interpretation of Isaiah's prophecy and was also probably quoting an opinion that was common among the
leaders of the Christian community in his day. If he and
they knew that this prophecy gives believers the legal
right to claim healing, then why didn't they say so?

The coming of the kingdom

The gospel of Matthew is also preoccupied with the
theme of 'the kingdom'. This is seen again and again in
the way it records the parables (see Mt. 13:11,19,24,31,33
etc). Jesus made the kingdom of heaven his principle
message when he was engaged in his healing missions
(Mt. 9:35). In fact, the twin terms 'the kingdom of God'
and 'the kingdom of heaven' are found between them
over eighty times during the gospel accounts of the ministry of Jesus.

The meaning of the term 'the kingdom' in Matthew
appears to have two dimensions. One refers to the

Second Coming of Christ, as in chapter 25, whilst the other appears to be realisable now in both space and time (Mt. 9:35; 10:7; 12:28). These two aspects of the one subject are important and teach us what George Ladd calls the 'now and not yet' of the kingdom.[28] We have some of the benefits of the kingdom right now but not all. This is seen in the fact that we are not yet one hundred percent free from sin – as anyone involved in local church life can tell you. Also, we still die, even though the abolition of death once and for all is a part of the gift of the kingdom of heaven. The New Testament clearly portrays the full coming of the kingdom of God as a future event. The return of Christ – the consummation of the kingdom – is shown to be imminent: it is not here yet but could happen at any time. Now is the time of the betrothal but the wedding is still to come (Rev. 19:7). We are called now to enter the kingdom of God through faith, but entry into the kingdom of God in its fullness is in the future (Mt. 25:34). Meanwhile we are called to live in the light of the coming of the kingdom in its fullness and to enter in to the works of the Holy Spirit as the kingdom grows amongst us now.

Robert Hillman was a preacher and writer who exercised a profound healing ministry even while he battled with the storm of terminal illness that finally claimed his life. He wrote

> Because we are living in the 'now and not yet' time, those who pray for the sick in a ministry of healing may observe a whole range of responses. Some people will be healed instantaneously just as in New Testament times. Some will be healed progressively, some partially, some temporarily and some will not be healed physically at all. Whatever the degree of healing, whether healing occurs or not, we are more likely to be able to minister

appropriately if we have a sound understanding of kingdom theology – if we understand that *the signs of the kingdom are with us but all has not yet been perfected.'*[29]

Some attempts to understand the kingdom teaching of the New Testament make the mistake of leaning too far either one way or the other. Either they offer a 'realised eschatology' where the entire kingdom is already present (as do Urquhart and Hagin) or else they write off all the works of God's power connected with his kingdom to the end of time with no current application available. We need to avoid both of these two extremes if we are going to understand Matthew's purpose (and through him the Holy Spirit's intention) in making the comment that he does in 8:17, and if we are going to grasp some of the potential answers to the question as to why we see some signs of the kingdom now, but not all of them.

The significance of the Lord's Prayer

Jesus taught his disciples to pray 'Your kingdom come, your will be done on earth as it is heaven.' Why would he do that unless he felt that through prayer we could experience more of God's heavenly kingdom in our lives than we are doing at present? He doesn't say how much of the kingdom will come now if we pray, but he does encourage us to ask for it and to do so with confidence and faith.

As we have seen, some faith teachers criticise those praying for healing for using the words 'Your will be done' saying this indicates a lack of faith. As one such website puts it 'the person who prays for healing, adding the words, "If it be thy will" is openly confessing to the Lord that he is not at all sure he will receive healing. The "if" in the petition denotes doubt. This type of prayer cannot possibly be classified as asking "in faith, nothing wavering." Praying this way for one's healing is a waste of time . . .'[30] Yet Jesus gave us the words and they are a sign of God's desire that we should pray his future kingdom blessings into reality now. He also used the words himself when he prayed 'Father, if you are willing, take this cup from me; yet not my will, but yours be done.' Jesus did not presume on his Father's will at that stage, despite all the Scriptures that pointed to it. Rather, he submitted himself to it with these words. If he did so, then so should we.

In Ephesians 1:11–14 we have some helpful teaching on this subject. In verse 14 Paul states that we have been given the Holy Spirit as a 'deposit guaranteeing our inheritance until the redemption of those who are God's possession – to the praise of his glory.' What Paul does not make clear is how big the deposit is. When you buy a house in Britain, for instance, you usually put down a deposit of between five and ten per cent as a sign of good faith and a commitment to pay the rest upon completion. That deposit becomes the guarantee that the rest is coming. In the kingdom of heaven, we are not told how much the deposit is – is it ten, twenty or thirty per cent?

We don't know. What we do know is that there is a deposit and that is ours now and that the full amount will be available at the time of completion (at the end of the world as we know it) but is clearly not available yet. This is one of the reasons why Christians still get sick and die and why some prayers seem to remain unanswered. So, instead of making unhelpful demands based upon wishful thinking rather than biblical teaching, let's keep praying 'Your kingdom come' and look for the deposit to be fulfilled among us.

The meaning of Matthew 8:17

The plain meaning of the text relates to the healing activities of Jesus in Galilee as referred to in the surrounding passage and not to the work of Jesus on the cross. As one New Testament scholar and commentator on the gospel, Alan McNeile, notes 'Matthew, or his source, makes no reference to the propitiatory value of the Servant's work; he quotes the wording of it mechanically, to illustrate the immediate incident . . . The passage, as Matthew employs it, has no bearing on the doctrine of the Atonement.'[31]

The use of the extract from Isaiah 53 in Matthew 8:17 refers to the healing ministry of Jesus in the region of Galilee. It does not anticipate the effects of the cross. To say that it does is to read something into the text that was not there in the first place. For Matthew it was plain that the healings of Jesus came from God and so it was natural to find them prophesied in a scriptural passage that clearly also came from God and had authority among the Jewish folk of his day. Jesus removed our sicknesses by healing them when he was on earth ministering in the power of the Holy Spirit in Galilee, as he still does today occasionally through the prayers of his people and the gifts of his Holy Spirit.

Simon Peter was as close to the Lord as any of the early disciples, closer than many of them. What did he say about the subject of whether healing is available in the atonement? One of the most quoted verses used in support of that teaching comes from Peter's first epistle and it is vital to consider.

A closer look at 1 Peter 2:24

> 'He committed no sin and no deceit was found in his mouth.' When they hurled their insults at him, he did not retaliate; when he suffered, he made no threats. Instead, he entrusted himself to him who judges justly. He himself bore our sins in his body on the tree, so that we might die to sins and live for righteousness; by his wounds you have been healed. For you were like sheep going astray, but now you have returned to the Shepherd and Overseer of your souls (1 Pet. 2:22–25).

In this passage there are no less than five quotations from, or echoes of, Isaiah 53. Verse 22 follows the form of Isaiah 53:9, with 'He committed no sin and no deceit was found in his mouth'. Verse 23 offers a parallel of Isaiah 53:7, 'He was oppressed and afflicted, yet he did not open his mouth'. Verse 24, the verse in question, repeats terms taken from Isaiah 53:12, with 'He himself bore our sins in his body on the tree' and, most significantly for the subject in hand, from Isaiah 53:5, 'by his wounds you have been healed'. Finally, in verse 25, Peter recalls the text of Isaiah 53:6 with his 'For you were like sheep going astray'.

Did Peter teach healing in the atonement?

Was it Peter's intention to teach here that physical healing is in the atonement on the same basis as forgiveness? Nowhere in the Acts' record of Peter's preaching did he mention that, so did he do so here? Some preachers and teachers believe that he did, so does the evidence of that stack up? It is necessary for those who proclaim this doctrine to prove that their use of this verse is correct.

If that is what Peter meant, then the context would certainly support it. The verse in question (1 Pet. 2:24) is set in a passage that addressed the problems being faced by Christians who were or had been slaves. It comes in a wider section from verse 13 that talks about submission to rulers and authorities, and some commentators believe that Peter was aware of how hard that might be for slaves.[32] He would have guessed that they were suffering under the harsh demands of a regime into which they had been placed against their will. They didn't choose their circumstances, nor is it likely that they enjoyed their work and some of them may have been suffering even more intensely since they had become Christians. There would have been a sense of unfairness in their hearts about their situation and that would have added to their pain.

Peter wanted them to know that the Lord Jesus knew about how they felt and had in fact been there before them. It must have been very difficult for them to get the time off to gather with other believers. Some may also have suffered persecution because they would not engage in some of the more sinful and degraded aspects of licentious first century living. So, in this passage, Peter calls the Christian slave to endure unjust suffering, following in the footsteps of Christ. As Michael Ramsay points out in the *Word Biblical Commentary*, Peter holds up before them the behaviour of Jesus in the face of his own terrible suffering as a model that these Christian slaves should emulate – and not just them, but suffering Christians everywhere.[33] In verse 22 the writer's intention is to show that Christ committed no offence to justify the sufferings inflicted upon him. He was the ultimate innocent victim of abuse. So in that sense the context is not about physical healing.

Philip Greenslade says in his commentary that in these verses Peter has one eye on the pressure his readers are facing, notably those who were slaves in first century households, and one eye on the suffering Christ.[34] In that vision, found in verses 24–25, the apostle exalts in the spiritual power of the cross. The cross removes the burden of our sin – 'He himself bore our sins . . .'; the cross renews our life – '. . . that we might die to sins and live for righteousness . . .'; the cross restores our relationship with God – '. . . you have returned to the Shepherd and Overseer of your souls'. In the middle of this joy about our spiritual redemption, Peter takes up the words of Isaiah and declares 'by his wounds you have been healed'(1 Pet. 2:24c). As Greenslade says 'Salvation is for us the recovery of our spiritual health. And this is what the cross achieves.'[35]

Peter's quotes from Isaiah 53 are not strictly a word for word repeat of the Greek Septuagint translation of the Old Testament. This may have been because he was quoting from memory, or using the familiar words of an early hymn. If this was part of the worship and musical tradition of the Early Church, then the words and concepts would be well known by the readers and applicable to the wider Christian community. In the first phrase of verse 24, Peter moves from the second person to the first person plural for the first time since 1:3: 'He himself bore *our* sins in his body on the tree' (italics mine). By doing this, he shifts the reader's focus so as to bring into view all believers, irrespective of their social standing, male or female, Jew or Gentile, slaves or free. In the words 'by his wounds you are healed,' Peter adapts Isaiah 53:5, using physical healing as a metaphor for spiritual conversion and recovery. But why would Peter use the word 'healed' in this verse if he did not mean physical healing?

The word used for 'healed' in 1 Peter 2:24

Peter used a word here that had become interchange-able for both physical healing and figurative healing, including forgiveness and restoration. The Greek word for healed used here is *iathete*, which is derived from the verb *iaomai* which is itself the origin of the word *iatros* – the name for a physician. In the New Testament *iaomai* is used less frequently than *therapeuo* (from which we get our English word therapy) when referring to physical healing. There are only a few scattered references in the epistles – there is a lot less material about healing in the epistles than there is in the gospels and the Acts – where a word for healing is required. In each case, the word *iaomai* or one of its derivatives is used (1 Cor. 12:9,28,30; Heb. 12:13; James 5:16; 1 Pet. 2:24).

In the pre-Christian era, the word *iathete* was used to denote healing from physical sickness and occurs as early as Homer's *Iliad*, around 800BC. But in Jewish writings of the inter-testamental and New Testament period, the word began to take on the concept of figu-rative healing, including forgiveness and restoration. In the twenty-six times the word is used in the New Testament (including words derived from it) both meanings are possible and it is the context that every time must determine the correct one in any given text. In the Early Church, both uses of the word can also be found. The context of the passage in 1 Peter, however, does not require that the physical meaning should take priority. In other words, the interchangeable meaning of the word does not allow this to be a proof text for the healing of physical sickness in the atone-ment.

Let the Bible interpret the Bible

So we can see that neither New Testament commentator on the prophecy of Isaiah understood it to be a legal statement regarding the right of every sick believer in Christ to be healed. As Gordon Fee, a Pentecostal theologian and writer, put it

> Matthew clearly saw Isaiah 53:4 as referring to *physical healing* but as a part of the Messiah's ministry not as a part of the atonement. Peter, conversely, saw the 'healing' in Isaiah 53 as being metaphorical and thus referring to the healing of our *sin* sickness. Thus neither New Testament reference sees the 'healing' of Isaiah 53 as *referring to physical healing in the atonement.*[36]

If the Bible writers themselves did not understand the texts as meaning that physical healing is in the atonement, to be claimed by believers as a legal right, then no wonder they said nothing about it in their preaching. The proof that the 'healing is in the atonement' teachers require from the New Testament key verses simply is not there.

Chapter 8

Why Did Jesus Die? – A Definition of the Atonement

In Romans 5:11 the Authorised Version uses the word 'atonement' but the NIV and other more recent translations use the word 'reconciliation'. 'Not only is this so, but we also rejoice in God through our Lord Jesus Christ, through whom we have now received reconciliation'. That change of words reflects the true meaning of atonement – reconciling a sinner with God. Whilst the word itself is not prominent in the New Testament (it appears just three times in the NIV New Testament) the concept or theory of atonement clearly is.

It derives from Old Testament thinking, particularly with regard to the Jewish practices surrounding the Day of Atonement, Yom Kippur, a very important part of the Jewish religious calendar to this day. The Hebrew verb *kapar* from which Kippur derives is generally used to mean 'to atone, to wipe clean or to appease.' So when Jacob wanted to appease his brother Esau's anger in Genesis 32:20, he sent a huge gift of livestock and goods on ahead of his expected encounter with him – to wipe the past clean and to appease his brother's anger. The word *kapar* is used again in Proverbs 16:14: 'a king's wrath is a messenger of death, but a wise man will appease it.' In Leviticus 16 where the instructions for the Day of Atonement are given to Israel, the word *kapar* is used sixteen times and the whole purpose of the proceedings was to clean up God's people from their sins and appease a holy God.

When we come to the New Testament the equivalent Greek word, though rarely used, has about it the whole idea of reconciliation to God. So in Romans 5 Paul refers to being 'justified by his blood' (v9) and that we have been reconciled to God by his (Christ's) death (v10). The language here is substitutionary, very much linked into the Old Testament concept of ritual sacrifice. Christ died in our place. He was the atoning sacrifice for our sins and the means of our reconciliation with God, through his death on the cross. Now none of this requires any involvement of sickness nor makes any provision for it, except in as much as when sin is finally done away with, at the Second Coming of Christ, all the consequences of sin will be finally eradicated too, including sickness.

A narrow definition

It is possible to define atonement in both a narrow and a broader way. In the narrow definition it is an act of reconciliation, where those who were in a state of estrangement become one with each other again. This would appear to be the sense of Romans 5:11 and is the reason why some writers try to define the word by breaking it down to 'at-one-ment'. It refers to the reconciliation between humanity and God brought about by sacrifice – the sacrifice of Christ on the cross. This narrow use of the term atonement relates to issues connected with sin. It is sin that has caused the separation between God and man, not sickness. The atoning work of sacrifice, therefore, in the setting of both Old Testament religion and the cross, relates to the reconciliation of God and sinful man, not upon sickness directly. As Gordon Fee points out

> In saying 'Christ died for our sins,' the creed[37] presupposes alienation between God and humans because of human rebellion and sinfulness, for which the just penalty is death. Death 'for our sins' means that one died on behalf of others to satisfy the penalty and to overcome the alienation. . . . the concept of substitution is woven into the very earliest of the Christian creeds.[38]

In referring to sin, we must not overlook the place of the consequences of sin. Sickness came into the experience of mankind through the fall in Genesis chapter 3 and so is a consequence of sin. There will be no sickness in heaven when the kingdom of God is fully come. We must be careful not to make from that the sweeping assumption that all sickness is to be regarded as the consequence of personal sin. The book of Job will not allow us to think like that, because Job's comforters were criticised by the Almighty for presuming that Job's sickness was simply caused by his wrongdoing. His so-called 'friends' were merciless in promoting their favourite theory, that goes like this:

- Good people = healthy people
- Bad people = sick people.

But the Lord said that they were badly mistaken. Their simplistic formula would not stand the revelation of God.

So, there is not much room for physical healing in the narrow meaning of the word 'atonement.' However, a wider view of the subject may be appropriate.

A wider definition

There is also a wider meaning to the word atonement, in which it is synonymous with all that Christ achieved by his work on the cross. This wider application of the word is apparent in both Church history and the New Testament. It includes such doctrines as propitiation, redemption and justification. The first uses imagery taken from the Jewish temple, the second from the marketplace and the third from a court of law, yet all reflect some aspect of the atonement. Much more can be understood about these terms from a study of John Stott's excellent book, *The Cross of Christ*.[39]

It is in this wider use of the term that some place may be found for the concept of healing through the atonement. This can only be true in so far as it includes aspects such as redemption (which Paul applies to the redemption of the body in Romans 8:23 in a passage relating to the Second Coming of Christ) or the victory of Christ over the powers of evil. In this latter regard, however, we need to set the victory of Christ within the tension of the 'now and not yet' of the kingdom of God. So neither the narrow definition of the atonement, nor a wider one, will allow for the teaching that physical healing is available in the atonement in the same way that reconciliation and forgiveness clearly are, except in a strictly eschatological setting.

If not now, when?

Following on from our look at the key texts in this issue
and in the light of the brief analysis of the New
Testament doctrine of atonement, we cannot escape certain conclusions. The first is that there is no exegetical
support for the claim that healing is unambiguously part
of the atoning work of Christ. When properly understood, none of the Bible passages supports the doctrine
that healing is our legal right now because of the atonement. Secondly, the theology of atonement itself makes
it unsuitable for application to the issue of sickness and
healing. Disease carries no penalty that must be atoned
for. So to equate the healing of disease with the forgiving
of sin, as Hubbard does,[40] is a mixing of terms – an unin-
telligible notion.

   Yet, despite having said that, there remains the nagging fact that there does appear to be some effect of
the cross which reaches beyond the issue of atonement for sin alone. On the very same page as his stout
rebuttal of the notion that Christ died for our sicknesses, Stott maintains 'that does not mean, however,
that our bodies are unaffected by the death and resurrection of Jesus'.[41] There does seem to be a link
between what Christ did on the cross and the healing
of the 'griefs' and 'infirmities' that arise out of our
being in a state of rebellion against God and his ways.
This leads to two possible conclusions. The first is that
physical healing comes to believers ultimately, when
after this life the full effects of the atonement are
realised in the kingdom of heaven. Secondly, healing
flows in an indirect way through the atonement of
Christ, in that the healing ministry of the Holy Spirit
is only available to the Church because of what Christ
did on the cross.

The ultimate solution

Physical healing of all disease will occur at the time of the Second Coming of Christ and our gathering together to him. In the few verses that follow Romans 8:18, Paul teaches that what he calls frustration and decay entered into the experience of creation at the fall of man recorded in Genesis 3. He sees this as the origin of sickness. He argues in 1 Corinthians 15:51 that full transformation of the body for both the living and the dead will happen at the Second Coming. Those believers, therefore, who are sick at the time of Christ's return, should certainly expect to be healed at the moment when 'the corruptible is clothed with incorruption'. For Paul, salvation meant ultimately entering the kingdom of God with a resurrection body adapted to life in that kingdom. The day when sin will be finally vanquished is the day when sickness will be utterly banished.

Andrew Brandon endorses this view with a simple analogy.[42] He sees the benefits secured through the death of Christ like a legacy left to a child. An allowance may be given to the child through their upbringing to cover certain expenses, but the full inheritance waits for the age of majority. Through the death of Christ, Brandon argues, God has provided a legacy of forgiveness and health and the abolition of death. Though we do receive parts of the legacy now, the fullness of this inheritance waits for the future hour when Christ shall come again.

There is a wonderful passage in Revelation 21:3–4 where the promise of a glorious day of freedom from pain is held out to those of us who struggle daily with it.

> And I heard a loud voice from the throne saying, "Now the dwelling of God is with men and he will live with them. They will be his people and God himself will be

with them and be their God. He will wipe every tear
from their eyes. There will be no more death or mourning or crying or pain, for the old order of things has
passed away."

It would appear, then, that there is no ground for believing in a direct link between healing and the atonement,
except in the sense of the ultimate restoration of all
things at the Second Coming of Christ. Is there, however, the possibility of there being some sort of an indirect link?

By indirect means?

In the New Testament healing is seen as the work of the
Holy Spirit. The miracles of Jesus began with his experience of the Spirit at his baptism and following his time
in the wilderness. The Early Church after Pentecost
began to experience healings and miracles as the Holy
Spirit worked among and through them.

When Paul wrote to the church at Corinth he listed
gifts of healings among his line-up of *charismata* – spiritual gifts (1 Cor. 12:9). Within the early Christian
community, it was the gift of the Spirit that became
recognised and acknowledged as the sure sign of God's
acceptance. This is why Peter could not refuse baptism to
the Gentile converts in the household of Cornelius who
had received the Holy Spirit just as he had on the Day of
Pentecost (Acts 10:44–48). The gift of the Spirit, and his
subsequent working through the lives of believers, was a
result of the justifying work of Christ on Calvary. Whilst
this seems a logical argument in itself, it is no more than
could be said for any of the benefits that flow into the
lives of Christians because of the work of Christ on the

cross. In that sense every good thing that we receive from God is an indirect fruit of the atonement.

The work of the Spirit in healing sick people today is a foretaste of the age to come, in which perfect healing will follow the removal of sin. It is a kind of 'first-fruits' or symbol of the final eradication of sickness to come at the time of the end of all things. In this sense, then, the work of the Spirit in healing is linked to the eschatological hope of total healing held out in the prophecy of Isaiah and elsewhere.

How come they get results?

Most folk who will take exception to what I have been teaching from the Scriptures here will point to the fact that those who do believe that there is healing in the atonement do seem to get results. Whilst some critics may denounce those claims of healing as spurious or short-lived, I disagree. There will always be the danger of exaggeration due to enthusiasm or claims made in the heat of the meeting which may not outlive it, but there are some healings that are genuine, lasting and provable. Just not enough of them! It is unacceptable to blame those who do not get healed. Neither is it right to denounce those who are healed as frauds or misled. What is going on?

Firstly, any healing that follows the laying on of hands and believing prayer of a committed Christian in the name of Jesus has to be credited to God's power, manifest in one way or another. It is his work and he should get the glory, not the one who prayed, the one who was healed or the organisation that put on the event. Secondly, any healing is a work of his grace. It is the use of the gift of the Holy Spirit who gives 'gifts of healings' (note the double plural) when the Church gathers. Thirdly, healings are a breakthrough of the kingdom of heaven in the here and now – those firstfruits of the harvest of which we have already spoken. They are signs that point to a greater reality – the eternal spiritual healing that is available in Christ.

In this sense, then, God is blessing the gospel message, not the messenger. It is certainly not an endorsement of everything that the messenger believes or teaches. The likelihood of error would be great if we did that. The Bible warns of the possibility of false miracles being performed to turn people away from Christ and truth. We should not be overly worried about this, as the fruit of any such healing will become clear in the life of the individual concerned. Jesus said 'by their fruit you will know them'. Our experiences, however grand, should never be allowed to dictate our understanding of the Scriptures, though it would be foolish not to expect them to be an influence. We must do our best to put that aside and ask the question 'Does the Bible teach that?' We do so for our own sake and for the sake of those as yet unhealed.

Conclusion

There are those who regard the atonement as offering healing on the same basis as salvation. Christ died for our sicknesses, they claim, as well as for our sins, so that there remains nothing left which needs to be done for both our salvation and our healing, apart from our faith. I have tried to answer the important question as to what extent healing is available through the atonement, if at all. There are no unambiguous exegetical grounds for believing that physical healing is available now through the atonement in the same way that forgiveness of sins certainly is. Indeed, if this were so, then why are the New Testament writings of both Peter and Paul so silent on the subject? Both men proclaimed forgiveness through the atonement (Acts 2:38–39; 16:31), yet said so little about healing.

The answer has to do with the relatively recent date for the origin of this particular teaching. These things were not taught by Jesus or his apostles because they are a recent invention. Peter and Paul did not preach this teaching because they did not believe it. Neither did the Early Church leaders. For a good review of what the Early Church Fathers wrote about the charismata in the first few centuries after the apostles, see Robert Dickinson's book *Does God Heal Today?*[43] It appears that there was no historical record of the healing in the atonement theory in that era.

The promise of physical healing, however, is linked to the coming of the kingdom of God. Whilst that kingdom is breaking in upon us now in present day occasional healings, it awaits fulfilment in a day that is yet to come. When that day dawns, death itself will be done away with forever as an effect of the ending of sin. Sickness will then be no more.

As we have also seen, physical healing is available through the work and ministry of the Holy Spirit today. The gifts of healings come to the believer because of the work of the cross but, more than that, they produce what Paul calls the 'firstfruits' of our inheritance. Such works of healing are forerunners of greater things to come.

In all this I have no desire to minimise the place of physical healing in the life of the believer or of the Church. Nor do I intend to deny the effect of the cross, which should be at the centre of our Christian life and experience. Yet an evaluation of the extent to which healing is available in the atonement may serve to take the pressure off those who suffer and remain unhealed despite their faith. It will also offer a theological and exegetical perspective to what has become an emotive issue.

As I was to find out, however, again and again through the last decade or so, some folk can't help making judgements about a person's faith, based on whether or not they are healthy. What right do they have to do that?

Chapter 9

The Shield of Faith

Does size matter?

How big does your faith have to be in order to be healed? Not very big, according to Jesus. 'I tell you the truth, if you have faith as small as a mustard seed, you can say to this mountain, "Move from here to there" and it will move. Nothing will be impossible for you' (Mt. 17:20). In fact, a tiny little bit of faith in a mighty God would seem to be able to work wonders. I often think about faith when I remember some of the rickety bridges we saw in Africa. These frail structures were sometimes stretched across spans of muddy water that became raging torrents in the rainy season and presented a challenge to faith. A lot of faith in a weak bridge would probably end up in disaster. No matter how much believing you try to do, if the structure is fundamentally unsound, you are simply not going to make it.

When we arrived back from Africa, however, and moved to Cardiff, we were presented with a very different kind of bridge. The two Severn crossings, both impressive motorway bridges transiting the estuary, are strong and capable structures. Here a tiny little bit of faith in a strong structure would see me safely across. So the issue is more about the strength of the bridge rather than the size of our faith. The teaching of Jesus implies that we must be careful where we put our faith and how we use it, rather than worry about the size of it.

The New Testament emphasises that faith is the opposite of works – with work you have to produce more and more to get rewarded but faith is the gift of God for those who ask for it. 'For it is by grace you have been saved, through faith – and this not from yourselves, it is the gift of God – not by works, so that no-one can boast' (Eph. 2:8–9). Yet sadly, for some Christians, faith has become a kind of religious work that we perform in our own strength and then present to God so that he can reward us with blessings or healing. The answer to prayer then becomes a kind of wage that is paid to a (literally) faithful employee. This is all wrong and is the opposite of what God intended.

Imagine the scene. A suffering believer comes staggering up to Jesus with a quantity of faith in his hand. 'Please heal me' he cries. Jesus stretches out his hand to receive the faith for examination and the sufferer hands over what he has brought. 'Pah, is that all you could find?' retorts an offended Lord. 'Off you go and find some more faith and when you have managed to acquire enough, come back to me with it and I will heal you.' Now if that scenario was true, and thank God it isn't, then the sufferer would be engaged in works – the activity of gathering sufficient faith. It is also the opposite of the kind of person the New Testament reveals Jesus to be.

Yet, suffering Christians are often depicted as being low in faith. I have had visiting pastors pray for me to have the faith to 'grasp my healing' and have even been asked by folk I have met if I have ever thought of trying prayer! There is a presumption in some Christian circles that if you are not healed it must be your fault, because you have not yet believed as you ought to have done. This happened to Gina and she wrote to me:

Hi Eric,

Tomorrow I go to the local general hospital for yet another endoscopic ultrasound to check on what the pancreas is up to now. I would like to share with you what happened last time – if you don't mind.

I have been to the endoscopic unit about twenty times or so in the last four years for botox injections into the pancreatic sphincter and sphincterotomies etc. Working there is a male nurse from Africa, who is greatly sought after by all the nurses and doctors alike as he has an uncanny ability to find veins for cannula insertion in problem patients like me with hardly findable veins. Last time as he quietly worked away he asked me if I had been ill for long. When I said for many years, he asked if it upset me to be ill. I then felt a bit uneasy and said I try hard to accept it as my lot, but I wanted to be well again. He then asked if I was a Christian and since I was, why did I not pray to be completely healed? I replied that if it was God's will, I believed I would be healed immediately, but that there must be a purpose in this illness. Because of this, I had to accept it.

At this answer, he said I had it all wrong. God loved me and would only want perfect health for one of his children. He asked if he could pray for me at his church that night and I said 'Yes.' He said the trouble with people in the Western world is that they no longer believe in miracles, so I had to go home and believe God would heal me and then I would be healed!

To be honest, I felt a bit vulnerable by then so just agreed I would do what he said. That was five months ago and I return tomorrow unhealed, feeling that in his eyes I am a failure and my faith is not strong enough. But on thinking about what you said, there is as much a miracle in still believing when you are not healed.

Some of my Christian friends were a bit angry at him but it was his way of belief and he was genuinely sincere. It will be interesting if I see him tomorrow. I think I'll tell him God is working on it. I know God has healed many aspects of my life and through my illness and the wonderful patients I have met in hospital wards he has brought me closer to him.

All the best, Gina[44]

Now from my previous correspondence with her I know that Gina is a Christian with a very sincere faith in God that has been sorely tried over many years of battling this dreadful disease. This was not the only time that she was made to feel guilty about not having enough faith to be healed, as there were other well-meaning believers who had put her in this frame of mind. Sometimes I think that my condition has taught me so much about God and brought me into contact with so many wonderful people, both as sufferers and in the medical profession. Like Gina, I have had real opportunities to get to know people I never would have done otherwise, to share God's word with them and to learn from them. In that sense, then, the illness, despite being a messenger of Satan sent to torment me (as Paul described his thorn in the flesh in 2 Corinthians 12) can be made by God to become almost an ally in our battle to serve the forces of light in a dark world. So faith does matter, but not in the way we sometimes think it does.

Faith under the microscope

Faith is vital. Without it we cannot know God or please him (Heb. 11:16) and it is by faith that Christians are justified – that is made clean from the guilt of their sins before a holy God, through the work of Christ done on the cross. So clearly it is not possible to be a Christian without faith. It is the lifeblood of a Christian profession, the underlying assumption of a Christian's personal story. Yet it is important not to elevate faith to a place that it does not biblically deserve. For instance, it is not right to focus on faith as the object of faith – to have faith in faith itself. If we do that, we are relying on works again – our faith has become a work with which we try to impress God. As in my illustration of the weak and strong bridges, what matters is who we are trusting in – and how strong he is – rather than the size of our faith.

Keith Warrington suggests that the kind of faith that Jesus commended was that which led people to believe that he could help them and to do something about it.[45] A simple declaration of trust in Jesus was enough for him to commend individuals for their faith. When Jesus commented on the absence of faith, he usually did so in circumstances where the lack of faith was being demonstrated by a rejection of him or his core message, an unwillingness to believe that he could or would help them. This happened at Nazareth, where the healing power of the Lord was restricted by the unbelief of the people (Lk. 4:16–30). Warrington argues that the unbelief expressed by the people in Jesus' home town should not be identified as limited faith in him, but as rejection of him.[46] His theory is that they were not questioning his ability to do miracles but, because of their intimate knowledge of him and his family, were choosing not to grant him the right to do them there. It is interesting, however, to note that even there in the atmosphere of unbelieving rejection, Jesus did do a few miracles. It is amazing to see the grace of God break through our human reluctance and even downright rebellion from time to time, like an overflow of God's compassion and mercy.

As Pete Greig, the leader of the 24/7 worldwide prayer ministry, says, 'Faith is not, as many people seem to believe, a transactional commodity we earn. Nor is it a spiritual currency with which we can acquire divine healing, provision or success. It is a relational posture of trust that enables us to receive the will of God in a way that others can't. Faith is a pair of open hands.'[47]

There were occasions when Jesus healed people without there being any mention of the person's faith. There was the occasion, for instance, of the healing of the woman with a bleeding condition that had plagued her for years, in which Jesus commended her for her faith (Mk. 5:34). That should be contrasted with a very similar healing in Luke 13:12–13 of a woman who had been bent double for many years, where there is no mention of her faith at all. Out of the 26 accounts of individual healing miracles recorded in the gospels, faith is mentioned in only twelve and amongst these there are eight in which it appeared that Jesus healed in response to faith. In only four of these it was the faith of the sick person to which Jesus responded, and in the other four it was the faith of friends or relatives that brought the commendation of Jesus.[48] Four out of 26 certainly takes the pressure off the sufferer, doesn't it?

So every time we come to Jesus, acknowledging that we are depending on him and seeking his aid, we are expressing faith. There were times, of course, when Jesus rebuked his disciples for their little faith. One example of this is found in Mark 4 where Jesus had been woken up by terrified disciples as they were crossing the Galilee in a small fishing boat during a storm. These followers of Jesus had become convinced that they were going to die even though Jesus was with them, asleep in the stern of the boat. When they woke him in a panic, they accused him of not caring about them: 'Teacher, don't you care if we drown?' (Mk. 4:38). It was this accusation that particularly stung Jesus as much as their unwillingness to trust that if he was with them, then all would be well.

Rising to the side of the boat, Jesus addressed the wind and the waves with the command 'Quiet. Be still!' Then there was calm. It was then that Jesus commented on their faith. However, the word that Jesus used to describe their faith was 'little' and is the same in the original Greek as the word that would be used to describe a young bird or chick. So he is rebuking them for their fledgling faith – not yet fully grown – rather than for the absence of faith. When we realize that, we can see that although our faith may not yet be as strong as it could be or perhaps as strong as it might become, it is stronger than it was. If it is even strong enough to bring us to the Lord with a sincere cry for help, then it is the real thing.

In addition to that, there is a strong commendation in the Scriptures for faith that perseveres under trial. Although it may take faith to receive a miracle and be healed, it also takes faith, perhaps even more faith – certainly of a longer duration – to keep trusting God in the face of repeated disappointments. This is the faith that is commended in the great 'hall of fame' of faith in Hebrews 11

> All these people were still living by faith when they died. They did not receive the things promised; they only saw them and welcomed them from a distance . . .

Women received back their dead, raised to life again. Others were tortured and refused to be released, so that they might gain a better resurrection. Some faced jeers and flogging, while still others were chained and put in prison. They were stoned; they were sawn in two; they were put to death by the sword. They went about in sheepskins and goatskins, destitute, persecuted and ill-treated – the world was not worthy of them. They wandered in deserts and mountains and in caves and holes in the ground. These were all commended for their faith, yet none of them received what had been promised (Heb. 11:13 and 35–39).

This is the kind of faith that I call 'third degree faith.'

Third degree faith

There are differing degrees of faith and different levels of God's active intervention in our lives. Does the apparent inaction of God on our behalf possibly signal a higher degree of faith even than that required to receive a miracle? Certainly there are times in our Christian walk when God appears to be silent or far away and we feel as though we are on our own. You probably know the poem *Footprints in the Sand* with its famous reminder that when there was only one set of footprints in the sand of our lives, Christ was carrying us and had not deserted us.[49]

The kind of faith that is needed to keep on believing and trusting when there is only one set of footprints and no obvious sign of the Lord's presence is persevering faith. I have called it 'third degree faith' because there appears to be at least two other degrees of faith. There is the faith that is the gift of God for salvation to all who believe (Eph. 2:8). Then there is the faith that grows through listening to God and reading his word and obeying what we see and hear (Rom. 10:17). In a sense both of these come from the Lord as gifts to his children. Persevering faith is also the gift of God to those who simply hang in there and choose to trust when everything seems to be going in the opposite direction to their expectations and hopes – that is faith to the third degree.

Lyn is a Pentecostal missionary working in Africa. She has known much blessing on her years of ministry there and in particular has seen many healings in response to prayer. Yet she tells of at least one occasion when all the praying for her desperately sick daughter did not prevent Lyn from having to leave her husband and the work and fly home to the UK to be with her. This is how Lyn reflected on the mystery of her situation in a periodical produced by her mission.

As Pentecostal Christians we believe in Divine healing . . . In Lubumbashi Congolese TV viewers are being healed as they watch the weekly 'Victory in Jesus' broadcasts, but not all our prayers for healing are answered immediately. God made a way for me to fly back to the UK at short notice, to be with my daughter Donna during a time of severe sickness. Why didn't God – who is all-powerful – just heal her so that my trip would have been unnecessary and my work here in Zambia uninterrupted? Donna was encouraged by some lines on a card from a church friend: 'Either your Father will shield you from suffering, or He will give you unfailing strength to bear it. Be at peace then and put aside all anxious thoughts.' One certainty, we are promised the peace of God in ALL circumstances.[50]

That is what I call third degree faith. It refuses to give up
on the hope of answered prayer and the expectation that
God still heals the sick, but it recognises that God is big
enough to make decisions for his own reasons that are
beyond our control and even our understanding.

In Pete Greig's book, *God on Mute*, this leader of a
worldwide prayer movement reflects on those times
when prayer simply does not seem to be enough. He
points out that Jesus knew unanswered prayer at least
three times in his earthly ministry.[51] The first was in
Gethsemane where he prayed for the cup to pass from
him (the answer did eventually come – it was no); the
second in John 17 where he prayed for all believers to be
one (definitely not happened yet) and finally on the
cross where he cried out 'My God, my God, why have
you forsaken me?' These prayers did not appear to have
been answered at the time they were prayed nor for
some time afterwards. The amazing thing about this fact
is that it puts the Son of God in our position too. It
means that there is a deep level of understanding in
heaven when, for whatever reason and there may be
many, our prayers have to go unanswered for a while.
When you think about it, the prayer of Jesus in John 17
that all his followers would be united has still not been
answered after two thousand years. That is persever-
ance.

Piling on the pressure

Third degree faith knows only one way to develop and
grow and that is through increasing pressure. It proves
its presence not by receiving its miracle but by receiving
instead the courage and trust to go through instead of
come out of its trials. Some of the world's most precious

commodities are found in the deepest and darkest places, where the pressure is immense. Diamonds, gold, silver, precious stones, uranium and coal are all mined by people working with great effort, at supreme risk and at great depth. In a similar way, third degree faith grows in the darkness, out of sight but certainly not out of mind and in places where the pressure is greatest, as we struggle to come to terms with or even to understand what God is doing in our lives. One of the greatest leaders of the Puritan movement in seventeenth century England, John Owen, wrote many remarkable books during his fruitful ministry, yet of his eleven children all but one died in childhood, two of the plague, and the daughter that outlived her teens died in her early twenties shortly after getting married. Owen did not give up trusting God. He pressed on as the recipient of third degree faith.

This kind of faith, like saving faith (Eph. 2:8), is a gift from God. It is the result of his love and grace towards us in Christ. It grows within as the fruit of the Spirit's presence, often only discovered in times of adversity. People sometimes say to me or to Diane, 'I admire your faith' when that faith is actually the result of God's work in us and he deserves our admiration. It is a kind of faith that is often not acknowledged by folk within what is sometimes known, ironically, as the faith movement. It may not move mountains but it does give the strength to climb a few.

Not long after the publication of my book *Braving the Storm*, a lady phoned to ask if she could come and see me. We had known Rose for many years and were intrigued when she said that she had to come and see us, rather than speak on the phone because she had read my book and wanted to give me something. When Rose came, I was in a lot of pain. It was one of those days when I had to resort to Fentanyl to control the pain level and it was not being particularly successful. So I was not really 'up' for a visit from anyone but curiosity, plus a love for Rose, made me willing to at least put in an appearance when I heard her voice downstairs greeting Diane.

Rose is one of those people who has also known a great deal of pain and sadness during her life but has continued to trust God through it all. She also has a real love of hearing from God through pictures, visions, words and prophecies.

'I don't want to disturb your rest' she began nervously, 'but I was at an event recently where some crafts were on display and when I saw this, I thought of you.'

'That's very kind of you' I replied, reaching out gingerly to receive the small plain cardboard box which she was offering me.

'I read your book with real interest' she said 'and I know how much pain you have endured and when I saw these on display I felt that they spoke to me of your life and all that you have been through.' By this time my curiosity knew no bounds and I quickly unwrapped the piece. There in my hand was a diamond shaped, hand crafted ornament made of cut glass crystal. Its facets all glinted with flashes of rainbow as they reflected and refracted the light of the sun.

'The Lord seemed to say to me,' Rose went on, 'that he was forming you into a diamond through the pressure of your many pains so that you would reflect his glory just like this crystal gleams in the light.'

By this stage, I felt suitably chastened that my pain had made me tetchy about receiving Rose and her gift, and that crystal now has pride of place in our home. Third degree faith is like that – formed in the darkness out of great pain and, when it is finished, it reflects the glory of the one who has allowed or even planned it, so that his light would be seen by those looking on. Thanks Rose!

Pearls of great price

I visited some friends in Guernsey not long ago who had been out fishing for ormers. These shell-fish, molluscs, are related to the abalones that are found in Australia and South Africa. In Guernsey, hardy individuals wade out into freezing sea-water at the lowest tides six times a year to turn over huge rocks and search for these highly prized gastronomic delicacies. My wife and I love them. Once the shell is removed, you beat them with a hammer on a stone pavement to make them softer to eat and then bake them slowly in the oven with butter, tomatoes, onions and herbs. Delicious! Our friends had taken pity on us because I was not well enough to go ormering myself and they had kept six of these fabulous molluscs back for us to enjoy. Amazingly, when they were cleaning them and removing the shells, a beautiful pearl fell out of one them, which they held up for me to admire.

Pearls are mentioned in the Bible – twelve gates to the city and each one of them made from a pearl. That's what John saw in Revelation 21:21 as he gazed by faith, and by special invitation of the Lord, at the eternal city that is to come. In other words, symbolically every entrance into the life of the heavenly city will be through a pearl. What is a pearl? Basically it is a healed wound. When oysters are bred for pearls, a wound is made in the shell and then a tiny grain of sand inserted. The irritant settles into the wound and then all the healing resources of this remarkable creature set to work and surround the intruder. As the layers build up over time, the grain of sand becomes a pearl, an object of exquisite beauty and value. Yet no wound, no pearl! So God does not waste our wounds and neither should we. My irritants can become his pearls. Heaven's gates will be a celebration of all the wounds God's people have suffered and he has turned into something of beauty.

Part Three

The Battle To Keep Believing

Chapter 10

Coping With the Unfairness of Life

Introduction

As I write this, a close Christian friend of mine, a wife and mother of three boys, two of whom have attention deficit disorder (ADHD) lies fighting for her life in a hospital ward following further surgery to remove cancer from her still young body. I am very unwell with chronic pancreatitis, another young couple in our leadership team have had a miscarriage and one of our elders has recently undergone a kidney transplant. Just an average week in a lively, growing church with a healing ministry!

In all this and in many other kinds of personal and communal disorders which afflict Christians as well as non-believers, like debt, unemployment, rebellious children, betrayal and divorce, we can find advice, wisdom, guidance and comfort in God's word. Nowhere is this more so than in the Old Testament prophecy of Habakkuk. If there is a phrase that sums up this Bible book, it would have to be 'Lord, it is so unfair!' Habakkuk was serving God at a time when it was deeply unpopular to do so. The people of Judah had been in rebellion against God and now they were about to be conquered by a heathen nation, the Babylonians from ancient Iraq. David Prior, in his commentary, sets the scene for us. 'Beginning with his own situation, he found himself articulating timeless questions – about the problems of evil and the character of God, about the apparent pointlessness of prayer and impotence of God, about the oppressiveness of unrestrained violence and the silence of God.[52]

Habakkuk's prophecy teaches us how to keep 'hanging in there' when the going gets tough. Out of the disaster of a sixth century BC conflict, there emerges a classic statement of believing trust and a song of confidence in God.

'It's so unfair Lord' (Hab. 1:1–5)

Complaining is an art form in contemporary British society. We complain about the weather, our health, the state of our communities and nation and we often complain about the Church. I recently heard a radio interview with the landlady of a north-eastern pub who tried to ban moaning and complaining until what she called 'the whingeing hour' straight after lunch on a Sunday. The idea became very popular and the pub was crowded every week for whingeing hour! Maybe there is something to be said for setting up a method for people to deal with their issues. That's what Habakkuk did with his complaints – he poured them out to the Lord. This is unusual among the prophets of the Old Testament who often reserved their darkest words for the king or for other prophets. In Habakkuk we are granted an intimate peek into the prayer life of someone arguing with God about his circumstances. Habakkuk found that there were great black holes of mystery in the universe of his walk with God and he wanted answers. Who better to turn to than God himself?

As we have seen, there are mysteries right at the heart of our Christian faith. Why should God's dear Son be 'despised and rejected by men'? Why is there a Roman executioner's gibbet at the centre of our worship and attention as believers? Why do good people suffer so much, when those of lesser scruples sometimes seem to thrive? Yet these are the facts and faith takes hold of the facts in one hand and the love of a sovereign God in the other and holds onto them both for dear life. You can throw as much research funding as you like at the mysteries of God and they will not necessarily either yield their secrets or go away. Philosophers agonise over them and theologians argue about them, but only God can make his ways known. Habakkuk decided that the path to understanding the answers that he sought was one of humble waiting on God.

Habakkuk prophesied in and around Jerusalem from approximately 609 until 605BC. The spiritual conditions described in verses 1–4 could not have occurred during the reign of the 'good' king Josiah, who died in 609, but do fit very well with the kind of things that were happening in the early part of the reign of his successor, Jehoikim. In his first chapter, Habakkuk is faced with a major ethical dilemma. He is concerned over the rampant sin and abuse of God's laws that was going on in Judah at that time. He wondered why God did not seem to do anything about it. God then informed him that he was about to do something amazing in response to all this wrongdoing, but that he would do so through a violent, evil godless nation called the Chaldeans (also known as the Babylonians). That led to Habakkuk's second dilemma – how could God do that? It was unthinkable that he would overlook the extreme evil of this fascist, violent society and use it to punish the people of God.

The first five verses of Habakkuk 1

> The oracle that Habakkuk the prophet received.
> How long, O LORD, must I call for help, but you do not listen? Or cry out to you, 'Violence!' but you do not save? Why do you make me look at injustice? Why do you tolerate wrong? Destruction and violence are before me; there is strife and conflict abounds.
> Therefore the law is paralysed and justice never prevails. The wicked hem in the righteous, so that justice is perverted.
> 'Look at the nations and watch—and be utterly amazed. For I am going to do something in your days that you would not believe, even if you were told.'

Clearly the tone is honest and disturbing. Habakkuk holds little back in his assessment of how things are around him. How does that compare with our prayers? How honest and real are we in our praying? I know that sometimes when I listen to myself praying I think that the person I am speaking to must be very important but extremely touchy! I go all around the bush to approach him carefully and then to set out my positive spin on what is going on in my life and his world. I know that we need to enter God's presence with praise and thanksgiving for who he is and that it does help to refocus our minds on the unchanging nature of God and to lift our vision above the circumstances that we are in. But let's get real. Sometimes the weight of the burdens we are carrying is too great and we ought to pour it all out to the Lord. As we have seen with anger, he can take it.

The word 'burden' is one that several of the Old Testament prophets used and it is clear that in these opening few verses of Habakkuk's prophecy he is carrying great psychological and spiritual weight. There are the dual burdens of the sins of the people on the one hand and the word of the Lord on the other. You get the feeling that if this man had not known God and his ways, then his confusion might not have been so great. After all, in Habakkuk 1:13 the prophet describes the Lord by saying 'Your eyes are too pure to look on evil; you cannot tolerate wrong.' If Habakkuk is then surrounded by evil and wrongdoing, where is God? The dilemma is a real burden prompting the prophet's outburst.

We need to take a moment here to uncover the danger of negativity and the difference between that and an honest and outspoken assessment of reality. The first may cause an unhelpful element of self-pity to creep in while the other is vital and is a sign of our maturity and wholeness. Whilst we do need to pour out our burdens before God, it would be good to avoid anything that would sap our strength and be an unnecessary burden.

The final chapter of the book of Jonah illustrates this difference between the two. It contrasts Jonah's negative emotions with the Lord's honest assessment of the state of Nineveh. Jonah was focused on the circumstances that he was facing and his own immediate comfort. God challenged him on his attitude and called him to try to acknowledge the bigger picture of what was going on around him.

It can be hard when we are expressing our darkest thoughts and fears before the Lord, but we must do so in a way that also allows him to speak to us in our spirits and through his word. Also when we go on to speak with others, there are issues which, like Mary the mother of

Jesus, we need to keep to ourselves and ponder in our own hearts. As Habakkuk was to discover in chapter 2, there can also be release in writing things down and keeping a journal of what God is saying and revealing. These simple steps may help us to keep being real whilst avoiding the perils of self-pity.

A tough world

If we make a list of the key words in the first five verses of Habakkuk, the list will include some remarkably similar things to today's newspaper headlines. Violence, destruction, injustice, strife, wrong, conflict, paralysed law, perverted justice and an unheeded cry for help are all there. Habakkuk has a keen sense of the holiness of God and is shaken by the sinfulness and appalling social conditions around him. Paul must have felt the same in first century Corinth or Ephesus, as we do today. Yet God had an almost outrageous solution to the problem in mind (see verses 5–6).

But whereas Habakkuk's cry was wrung from his heart by conditions in his land, ours may be formed by issues much nearer home. Physical or psychological pain may cause it, or maybe family or marital strife, church schism or even abuse of various kinds allowed or overlooked by church leaders. Our cry to God may be due to the corruption we may be aware of in our own community, or that which is preventing aid reaching far-off places.

So to a very small extent we can understand the kind of emotions that the prophet expresses in his opening verses of complaint before the Lord. What Habakkuk does for us in the early part of chapter 1 is to set out the process that leads to the song of faith and trust at the end of his book (Hab. 3:17–18). To go straight to that without attention to the due process could be glib and foolish. The prophet shows us the way to prepare our hearts for encouragement in a devastating situation. He shows us the value of lament.

Lament – the missing jewel in worship

A lament or lamentation is a song or poem expressing grief, regret or mourning. Many of the oldest and most lasting poems in human history have been laments. Laments are present in both the *Iliad* and the *Odyssey*, in the Hindu *Vedas* and in ancient Near Eastern religious texts. Much of the book of Psalms is lament – setting out sad things in poetry or song before telling of God's ability to meet the need. Psalm 73 is a case in point. King David was increasingly concerned about the fact that in his view the unrighteous and the ungodly seemed to get away with so much in life.

> Surely God is good to Israel, to those who are pure in heart.
> But as for me, my feet had almost slipped;
> I had nearly lost my foothold.
> For I envied the arrogant
> when I saw the prosperity of the wicked.
> They have no struggles;
> their bodies are healthy and strong.
> They are free from the burdens common to man;
> they are not plagued by human ills (Ps. 73:1–5).

Whilst we can see some exaggeration here – poetic licence perhaps – we can certainly understand the song-writer's dilemma. People who don't know God and follow his ways seem to do nicely, thank you. This fact was causing the writer's feet to slip, spiritually speaking. The lament has a definite turning point in verses 16–18

> When I tried to understand all this,
> it was oppressive to me
> till I entered the sanctuary of God;
> then I understood their final destiny.
> Surely you place them on slippery ground;
> you cast them down to ruin.

On this occasion the lament had an ending – a moment of revelation when the eternal dimension of the bad situation was made plain so that the one lamenting could go on following God and trusting in him. Yet with laments in the Bible, that is not always the case. Some of them are alarming, especially if you have a theology that includes an easy 'fix it' for every problem. Psalm 89:38–45 has a very honest outline of how things were in Judah at that time

> But you have rejected, you have spurned,
> you have been very angry with your anointed one.
> You have renounced the covenant with your servant
> and have defiled his crown in the dust.
> You have broken through all his walls
> and reduced his strongholds to ruins.
> All who pass by have plundered him;
> he has become the scorn of his neighbours.
> You have exalted the right hand of his foes;
> you have made all his enemies rejoice.
> You have turned back the edge of his sword
> and have not supported him in battle.
> You have put an end to his splendour
> and cast his throne to the ground.

You have cut short the days of his youth;
you have covered him with a mantle of shame.

That kind of song would probably not feature very highly in some contemporary worship leaders' lists but it should. Alongside the many songs that express good things, like looking up to God (rightly of course) and celebrating all the blessings that he has showered on us, there should be a place for lament.

It has always bothered me that if those who are suffering in any way come into our triumphalist celebrations, they will find no place to express their pain. Perhaps it is overlooked because of a theological viewpoint that cannot hold the reality of the goodness of God and of suffering in tension, so they hold to the first and try to ignore the second. Such an oversight dishonours God, his word and his world. Sin, disaster and chaos are aspects of this fallen world that he so greatly loves and has worked so hard to redeem. We should acknowledge that fact in our worship. Doing so would enable congregations to grasp a firmer handle on the truth that God is still in charge even in these kinds of situation. Such knowledge can be a saving grace in times of adversity.

The knowledge of the sovereignty of God has kept believers going in the most appalling circumstances – like Paul and Silas in prison in Acts 16. They learned to praise the Lord despite their conditions. At midnight, whilst sitting in the dreadful conditions of a first century Roman dungeon, their backs lacerated and bleeding, facing almost certain death, they sang hymns and praise songs to God. We don't know the content of their hymns but they may well have included psalms just like the ones we have referred to. Deliverance came to them in the form of an earthquake that opened the prison doors and – amazingly for an earthquake – snapped their chains! But they did not know that's how it would end when they chose to pour out their hearts to God at the darkest hour. We don't know how things are going to end either, but we must also choose to pour out our hearts, and lament may offer us a way of doing so.

I think that one of the reasons why we don't employ more lament in our worship, either corporately or privately, is that we have a fear of offending the Lord. It may also be because, as I pointed out in *Braving the Storm*, some Christians have a problem with being real. They choose rather to live in an evangelical 'la-la' land. Yet God is not shocked by our honesty but is concerned about our entering into denial, which would be a mistake. If ever we should be real, it is in the place of prayer.

How did Paul cope?

Wrestling with the problem of suffering is not only an Old Testament occupation. Despite all the healing miracles and amazing interventions of God in the gospels and the Acts, Paul and his team of Early Church planters faced exactly the same dilemma. Sometimes preachers today try to get around that fact by saying something like 'Ah yes, but that was persecution' as if that doesn't count in the summing up of suffering in our lives. Try telling that to an Ethiopian pastor shut up in a windowless container in forty degree heat for months on end, or a Nigerian Christian whose home and livelihood has just been burnt to the ground. I remember being in a prayer meeting when details of the persecution of the church behind the Iron Curtain in the communist era were explained, and one well-meaning old gentleman said out loud 'Oh, lovely suffering!' Was it lovely to those at the receiving end? No, their pain and Paul's was very real. Look again at the list the apostle gives

> Five times I received from the Jews the forty lashes minus one. Three times I was beaten with rods, once I was stoned, three times I was shipwrecked, I spent a night and a day in the open sea. I have been constantly on the move. I have been in danger from rivers, in danger from bandits, in danger from my own countrymen, in danger from Gentiles; in danger in the city, in danger in the country, in danger at sea; and in danger from false brothers. I have laboured and toiled and have often gone without sleep; I have known hunger and thirst and have often gone without food; I have been cold and naked. Besides everything else, I face daily the pressure of my concern for all the churches (2 Cor. 11:24–28).

Not all of those experiences were the direct result of persecution. I wonder how some preachers would handle the fact that Paul went without sleep, without food and was cold and naked at times? This hero of the faith did not live in abundance and prosperity all his days – except the spiritual kind that comes by virtue of the peace of God and the joy of the Lord. Elsewhere he laments that some of the churches he started had been unfaithful by failing to support his ministry financially and that others had even turned on him and refused to acknowledge him as an apostle at all. In 2 Corinthians 1:8 he makes a remarkable admission: 'We were under great pressure, far beyond our ability to endure, so that we despaired even of life. Indeed, in our hearts we felt the sentence of death. But this happened that we might not rely on ourselves but on God, who raises the dead.' It seems that Paul's conditions took him to the brink of despair, right up to death itself, and will have given him an understanding of those who have despaired of life because of suffering and pain.

There are many passages in the Pauline literature that give us insight into how he survived his ordeals. One of the best known is in Philippians 4. In it he reveals what he calls 'the secret of being content in any and every situation'. Contentment is a very precious commodity. It is much more than happiness and very different to resignation. It is a willingness to accept what is, however tough it may be, with a confidence that God is good and that he will eventually work everything out for his glory and our good.

Being content did not mean that Paul was coasting along in his faith. His contentment did not stop him longing for more of God and stretching for more in the kingdom of God, as is seen in Philippians 3:12–14 with his famous 'this one thing I do' speech. What being content did do for the man of God, however, was set him free from anxiety – particularly about money! I find that a challenge, because I do worry about money or rather the lack of it. But not so Paul. Whether well-fed or going without, he was at ease. He did not presume that God had abandoned him if things were tough. Whenever the word 'content' appears in Scripture, it is usually to do with money (1 Tim. 6:6–10, Heb. 13:5). The latter text adds the rider that we should be content with what we have 'because God has said, "Never will I leave you; never will I forsake you."'

So how do we get this contentment and what are its secrets? It is something we can learn only through the harder experiences of life. In Philippians 4 there are some keys:

- A personal relationship with Jesus Christ. Verse 13 says 'I can do all things through Christ who strengthens me'. These words were written from prison. It's the daily walk with Christ that matters to Christians in prison for their faith because they sometimes cannot meet with believers, yet the fellowship of the Lord's sufferings is constantly with them. It was his close relationship with Jesus that carried Paul through, together with his many compatriots in suffering.

- Rejoicing in the Lord in all circumstances (v4).
- Praying about everything with thanksgiving (v6).
- Refocusing the mind. We need to be focused on what is good and wholesome if we want to be content. This is the antidote to self-pity (vs 8–9).

Sometimes all the positive thinking in the world can't avert what you have to face the next morning, though.

Chapter 11

The Dilemma of Gethsemane

It was August 2005 and I was extremely uncomfortable, sitting in the middle of that vast crowd of people with a tube up my nose. Not that I wanted to be there in the first place, but I had no choice. I was in London facing major surgery to try and correct a blockage in my bile duct that was causing me major problems with cholangitis (a potentially life-threatening infection of the bile ducts) and pancreatitis – my old enemy.

I was checked in at the University College of London Hospital, near All Souls Church in Langham Place. I went there to attend the 6pm service. What drew me was that I had read that John Stott was to be the preacher that evening, a rarity since he was well into his eighties. These good intentions were confounded by the problem that I felt extremely weak and unwell and had not eaten or drunk anything for several weeks beforehand. I had been sustained by a tube. I felt very conscious of it, stuck as it was to my right cheek with sticky plaster. In addition, I knew that I was facing a massive operation the next day and was not sure that I would survive it. My prayer was something like this; 'Lord, if it is possible for this cup to pass from me without me having to drink it, then please, please let it do so.'

The pomp and skill of the All Soul's orchestra largely washed over me, though I found that the overall atmosphere did move me emotionally, despite the press of the crowd and my embarrassment. I was not prepared, however, for the shock of the Bible reading and the text that Dr Stott chose for his sermon. It was Luke 22:42: 'Father, if you are willing, take this cup from me; yet not my will, but yours be done.'

I don't think that I have ever felt so 'got at' by a preacher in my life as I did that evening, but in a good way. It was as if I was the only person in the huge auditorium and that while I was busily looking around at the imposing architecture, the preacher had come to the pulpit in what he thought was an empty church, took me by the lapels and led me to Gethsemane and I didn't want to go there.

I had been there before (Gethsemane that is) and I wasn't very impressed. For those who expect the garden of Gethsemane to be a manicured English Victorian set piece walled garden, it comes as a surprise to see the barren Middle Eastern scrub that it is today. The name 'Gethsemane' is derived from the Hebrew words *Gat Shemen* which mean olive press, a reference to the natural abundance of olive trees and to the presence of oil presses in the area. It is perhaps an ironic name given the pressure that was applied to Jesus there – squeezing out even sweat mixed with blood.

I have visited the real thing three times now and it always has the same effect on me – anticlimax. It is one of those places that you feel should be more than it is, given the significance of its role in the life of Jesus. Granted, the olive trees that are now propped up and wire-clad are reputed to have been there at the time of Christ but there is none of the sense of dignity and awe that this place should surely inspire. For here the Son of

God chose suffering and death over self-preservation and deliverance, for our sake. He could, as he claimed, have called legions of angels to assist him and to set him free from the evil clutches of the Roman torturers, but he refused to do so, preferring instead to suffer in our place.

In some ways, though it was called a garden, Gethsemane would have made a better crossroads. Even now hectic traffic rushes by within metres and carbon-laden fumes swirl around the olive groves. But then this was a crossroad of a different sort, a place of choosing which way to go in life, whose will to obey. On the one hand was the pressure of self-preservation that even the Son of God must have felt if he was truly also the Son of Man. Added to that very human emotion would have been the horror of Christ's divine nature at taking on the role of our substitute to face the wrath of God. On the other was the weight of love for lost people that called him to go on and become the sacrifice for sin that we all so badly required. He simply could not do what his Father was asking him to do and not go through with the pain that awaited him in the morning.

Although there was nothing vicarious about my suffering and certainly nothing substitutionary about my pain, I identified fully with the Saviour's dilemma that day in Langham Place. Presenting yourself for major surgery is probably one of the hardest – and loneliest – things that a person can do. Surgery is such savage mercy and the only way up is down. Even though you know that the outcome may well be helpful and positive, it is only natural to be apprehensive. I found great comfort that day in listening to John Stott as he spelt out what Jesus did for me. And I found myself facing the very same challenge as to whether or not I would be willing to go God's way and not mine. I knew that I had to choose to trust God and go forward holding onto him and his love.

Dr Stott dealt with the Gethsemane story as an illustration of what he called 'the integrated Christian'.[53] He was referring to the fact that we are only truly healthy when we have integrated body, mind, emotions and will, as Jesus did. In addition to the text chosen from Luke's gospel, he read the account from Matthew (Mt. 26:36–46). I was riveted by the preacher's exposition of the text, especially when he described the battle that goes on in our lives because of the strength of our personal will. Our own will so often collides with that of others – our parents, our teachers and others in authority over us – and frequently with God's. Gethsemane shows Jesus to be in the deepest possible human distress because of the realisation of what God was calling him to do and the battle of the will that was raging within.

Jesus sweated drops of blood (Lk. 22:44) because of the inner turmoil and agony taking place in his mind. He was possibly experiencing hematidrosis, an extremely rare clinical phenomenon caused by acute fear and intense mental concentration.[54] Was it the physical and mental assault that lay ahead of him from which Jesus shrank in Gethsemane? I don't think so. If you take a look at the tremendous courage and dignity that he had shown when undergoing personal physical attack before, such as at Nazareth near the start of his ministry, it is hard to believe that the prospect of physical suffering alone was enough in itself to cause this great anguish. Also, Jesus himself had warned his disciples that they would suffer in this world, even to the point of martyrdom, but that they were not to be afraid, for he had overcome the world. No, Jesus wasn't nervous of the pain that he was about to experience. Rather, he was deeply and emotionally affected by the knowledge of what, in the will of God, he was about to become – our substitute. It was this prospect of becoming an offering for sin from which Jesus recoiled.

At the centre of his dilemma that night in Gethsemane stood the question of the will of Jesus. Perfect God and perfect man, he was possessed of a fully formed human will. He had to choose to drink the cup, he would not be force-fed. It is, at the moment, illegal in any UK jail to force feed a prisoner. Only in a psychiatric institution can this be done in circumstances where it is legally presumed that the person is no longer in full possession of their mental faculties. Where there is a clear will to live or to die, to drink or not to drink, the law no longer forces a convicted criminal to do so against their will. So it was with Jesus.

He was a prisoner of the will of God and his love for sinful mankind. He knew the plan that his Father had resolved with him before the foundation of the world, that he should come into a sinful world, live a sinless life and then volunteer to become a sin-offering for all who believe and are justified by that faith. He must have withdrawn from the horror of all that lay ahead, and his love for the Father made the choice more bearable, but the decision to go through with it was still his to make.

Thankfully for all of us and the millions who have trusted in his work on Calvary down through the centuries, Jesus came to a place of resolution in this dilemma. Within a very short time of his agony in Gethsemane, he stood facing the arresting officers who had come out of the city with Judas. Simon Peter, with typically impetuous zeal, attacked the servant of the High Priest, cutting off his ear. 'Shall I not drink the cup the Father has given me?' was the Lord's rebuke (Jn. 18:11). He knew that the cup was now pressed to his lips.

In a much smaller and less spiritually intense way, that was my dilemma too and still is. The cup that I have been called to drink from was to contain more than a decade of intense suffering and long periods in hospital.

In fact, during the years following my first attack in 1997, I was to fly to the UK for medical purposes more than fifty times, often with an ambulance to transfer me from the local hospital in Guernsey to the runway, and from the terminal at Gatwick to the hospital in central London, sometimes with a qualified nurse in attendance. This was not my plan.

I had been leading a flagship, city centre Pentecostal church with a huge and growing following and a thriving ministry when I became ill. My plan involved preaching and teaching the Bible to others, leading the local church and training Christian leaders. God's plan seems to be a cupful of agony, blood, fever, sorrow, disappointment, loneliness, embarrassment and grief. Your circumstances may be much worse than mine but I am pointing out the contrast between what I wanted God's cup for me to contain and what it eventually did pour out for me. And there's the rub.

We are not in charge of our lives as committed Christians. God is and his ways are not the same as our ways (Is. 55:8). You might have wanted your cup to be full of happy laughing children in a loving Christian marriage and instead it has been filled with loneliness and singleness. Or, even worse perhaps, it has been the sting of bitter rejection and betrayal after a failed marriage and the stigma that it inevitably seems to bring with it, however unjustly. You may have planned that your cup would be filled with sacrificial missionary service for the sake of others and the building up of God's kingdom, but in the end it was stained with illness and rejection by mission agencies and churches.

Our dear friend Annette set off in Christian service some years ago to attend a Bible College in preparation for a lifetime of missionary work. She served for some years afterwards with the Evangelical Alliance at their headquarters in London and then went to Nepal as a missionary. Sadly, her time there was not an easy one and she returned to the UK after a couple of years, deeply traumatised by some of her experiences. Then, before the age of forty, she had a stroke and remains nearly totally incapacitated by its after-effects. The stroke happened shortly after she had taken a whole day of prayer to offer herself fully for the service of God. Her cupful was nothing like what she expected. It is in stories like hers, told and retold thousands of times in different circumstances, that the real dilemma of Gethsemane is seen for what it is. Jesus, God's Son, was identified with us totally in our struggles and pain. He drank his unique cup down to its last dregs so that we might be able to drink our own.

What shall we do with this will of ours?

Dr Stott was encouraging with his teaching that the human will is the result of God's own creative work in human beings. This means that there is nothing inherently evil about it. It is a normal part of human experience to both have a will and be called to exercise it regularly. The will is an act of creation: we are made to be fully self-conscious and self-determining as creatures. We are responsible for the decisions of our will, but behind our will, he explained, lies our fallen sinful nature. When he said that, I remembered the words of the apostle Paul in Romans 7:18–19 and they made new sense: 'I know that nothing good lives in me, that is, in my sinful nature. For I have the desire to do what is good, but I cannot carry it out. For what I do is not the good I want to do; no, the evil I do not want to do – this I keep on doing.' Dr Stott, in his sermon that day, skirted around the thorny subject of how our free wills might work when seen in the light of God's sovereignty and foreknowledge. He simply said that both aspects of Divine sovereignty and human responsibility should be held in an important balance as a mystery held in tension, but that should not detract from the important question of what we should do with our human will.

I listened hungrily to what he had to say next. I was by now very keenly aware of the battle going on in my own will as I faced the surgery in the morning. I wanted to know how to handle it – how to overcome the very real wrestling match going on in my emotions. He suggested that we should surrender our will to God. He pointed out that this is precisely what Jesus did throughout his life. From the moment when the Lord reminded his parents that he should be about his Father's business (Lk. 2:49) he had shown a desire to serve his heavenly Father's will above his own. In John 5:30 Jesus characterised his ministry when he said 'I seek not to please myself but him who sent me.' In John 6:38 he made his own position crystal clear: 'For I have come down from heaven not to do my will but to do the will of him who sent me.'

That was the point at which I stopped writing and started thinking deeply about what was being said. Yes, that's it. If God is my loving heavenly Dad and cares about me in the same way as I care about my own son Matthew, then I needed to trust him for the morning that was coming and let go. In both the prayers recorded in Matthew 26:39 and 42, Jesus begins with the words 'My Father'. The cup was to be seen as a gift from his Father, however awful it must have seemed. It was this assurance of the Fatherhood of God and his desire for his children's ultimate good that enabled Jesus to embrace his Father's will that night, dark and difficult as it was.

Towards the very end of his sermon, Dr Stott urged us to surrender our will to God and embrace his loving purpose in our lives, even if we could not understand it. So we came to the end of the message and the frail but awesome old man descended from the pulpit. And I prayed.

It was not the prayer that I had expected to pray. What I wanted to pray was a scream at the top of my voice 'Please, Lord, heal me now!' But instead I bowed my head in that great church and with my tears running down the side of the nasal tube taped to my face, I prayed with a better understanding 'My Father – my dear heavenly Dad – if it is possible, please let this cup of tonight's pain and tomorrow's terror pass from me . . . Yet, not my will but your will be done in my life.' And I felt the hand that brushed my tears away was not my wife's, but that of Jesus, whose hand was marked with the scar of his own agony as he sympathised with me in mine.

Chapter 12

Embracing the Cross

Suffering is at the heart of the Christian faith and cannot be avoided by those who follow a crucified Saviour. Yet, as a leader in the Pentecostal/charismatic tradition of the Church, I have felt for some time that we lack a coherent theology of suffering in our teaching. It is coming, largely because of the pressure of unfulfilled expectations and also from mature reflection upon God's word. Nevertheless it is not widely articulated because it is thought to be the prerogative of those who do not believe in healing or expect miracles to happen today. It is as if there are two camps among Christians – the faith camp and the unbelieving camp – those who believe it is God's will to heal the sick and those who aren't sure. What is needed is a balanced view that celebrates the healing power of God today and yet embraces the understanding that God can, in his sovereignty, choose to use suffering for his purposes. To be honest, this is all a bit mysterious – and that's how it is meant to be.

The place of mystery in our walk with God

One of the aspects of the lively sort of evangelical faith that I have known since my conversion to Christ during my teens is the confidence and boldness that comes from a personal encounter with the Holy Spirit. It is clear from the New Testament that such experiences in the lives of the earliest Christians had very similar effects upon them. From being timid and afraid of the Jews, they suddenly burst forth in bold proclamation of the gospel and the certainties of what God had done for them in Christ. It was the power of the Holy Spirit that made the difference. Yet these very same early believers had a respect for the mysteries of life and godliness – whole areas of their experience and faith where their questions went unanswered and their knowledge of what God was doing was incomplete.

This respect for mystery is clear in Paul's letter to the Colossians (1:24 – 2:3). The word 'mystery' is used three times here. It's a word we don't like because we want to understand things and we are impatient with it. Part of our educated Western culture means that we baulk at anything we cannot understand and research it until we do. If we cannot do that, then we expect that someone else should and explain it to us. There is little or no room in our worldview for mysteries. Yet the New Testament speaks often about them. In Colossians 1:27, for instance, the fact that Christ lives in us is a mystery. 1 Timothy 3:16 tells us that the gospel itself is a mystery ('the mystery of godliness'). The relationship between Christ and his Church is a mystery (Eph. 5:32), as is that between a husband and wife. Most of us who are married would add an 'Amen' to that idea! The coming rapture of the Church is also held up as a prime example of mystery in 1 Corinthians 15:51.

It's important for us is to notice how the word mystery is used in its Christian context, as against its common use in the religious and philosophical world into which Christianity was born. In these religions, there were many secrets which were only made known to initiates and kept hidden from others. That is not how the word *mysterion* is used by Christian writers. Their emphasis is that what is hidden and unknown about God and the universe can be made known to us in Christ. In the kingdom of God, a mystery is not a secret made known to the clever and privileged few, but rather insight that grows out of a level of trust and understanding that comes through an intimate and deepening experience of Jesus Christ, 'in whom are hidden all the treasures of wisdom and knowledge'.

Learning the answer to a mystery, then, does not come from human intellectual or philosophical achievement but rather from the revelation that flows from God to those who are in a relationship with Jesus. It is also something which can be grasped by a little child – anyone who can draw near to the Lord. Some of those who teach within the healing and prosperity movement make the same mistake as the Early Church Gnostics I mentioned before, who were a Christian sect who claimed special insight and superior knowledge not given to ordinary believers. Modern-day Gnostics sell their books and other media very effectively, as we have noted before, on the basis that they alone have the secret to healing, deliverance or other answers to prayer which is not generally known about in the Church. In adversity, we do well to avoid such material as this is not the Bible meaning of the word mystery.

'The way in which God governs his universe and cares for his children during this present "time between the times" is full of mystery' writes Robert Hillman.[55]

And so it is. There are countless examples where people have trusted God for healing and received it in ways beyond their understanding and ours. Yet alongside them there are equally precious and faith-filled individuals who do not seem to be healed or even relieved of their pain, despite all the praying and trusting by them or their loved ones on their behalf.

Our faith needs to be big enough to admit there is mystery and to still make Jesus Lord of our lives even in the midst of our confusion. Only then will life begin to make any kind of sense. It will also help us in accepting the reality of mystery if we come to understand certain truths about God: that he knows what he is doing, that he is bigger than we think and that he loves us more than we can ever understand.

God knows what he is doing

There was an international chess tournament in Guernsey not long ago in which the visiting chess master challenged the best of the local players to take him on – declaring that he would play blind-folded! Amazingly he did just that and did not lose a single match. Even though he could not see the whole board he must have memorised it in his mind from the moves that were made and announced as they happened, so that he built up a mental picture of the state of play. To a certain extent, the existence of mystery in our experience is a call from God for us to admit that we cannot see the whole board – but he can. He knows the plays that have been made and understands them perfectly, but he is also aware of the plays that will be made and which will impact on us in the future. 'He knows the end from the beginning': God knows what he is doing.

Accepting that there are mysteries is simply an admission that we don't know it all. That offends our pride, but it is a fact. Read again Isaiah 55:8–9: 'For my thoughts are not your thoughts, neither are your ways my ways,' declares the LORD. 'As the heavens are higher than the earth, so are my ways higher than your ways and my thoughts than your thoughts.' This kind of mystery came home to me more clearly when I received a letter from Kelvin following my visit to his church.

'Our God is a God of glorious mystery . . . unfathomable, immeasurable, inscrutable. Never can we do more than Moses and just catch the faintest glimpse of his back as he passes by. I was at a meeting where Mike Springer was speaking on evangelism. Just before he began to talk, though, he said, 'I believe God wants to heal some people. I believe there are some people here suffering from . . .' and before he completed the sentence I knew he was going to say 'asthma' and my hand was high in the air waving enthusiastically.

He came and prayed over me and while I could not at the time notice any physical change (I had been sitting peacefully for some while and my breathing was already settled), I did experience a deep sense of being incredibly loved. Later on in the meeting, many others were prayed for and at one point Mike said, addressing some of us, 'Of course, you may not even be in a position now to *know* if you've been healed. You may need to wait and see if the symptoms recur at times they normally would.' I replied, 'Well, there is a way I could find out. If I go down those two flights of stairs and come up again, everyone at the Tuesday prayer meeting will know the normal state I arrive in, having come up those stairs.'

At this point I went off to the bottom of the stairs and then ran straight back up . . . taking two stairs at a time! It's true I was a little out of breath as I burst back into the meeting room, but with none of the usual asthmatic tightening and closing of the airways and the fact of the matter was that, before the meeting, I couldn't have got close to doing it at all, without collapsing after half a dozen steps. There was absolutely no doubt in my mind, or the minds of those who knew me well, that I had been miraculously healed.

The following day, however, I wasn't. I had decided to stay off my medication until any symptoms began. It was safe enough to do this as my asthma invariably sets in slowly and I get plenty of advance warning. By that afternoon, though, I was back to needing my normal level of medication. I had without doubt had a healing experience the previous evening, but equally certain was the fact that I was no longer healed. My position seemed very confusing and inevitably I was peppered with doubts, questions and even guilt over the next few days.

I hesitated about going to the church meeting on Sunday where I knew, after such a dramatic and public healing, people would be asking me how I now was. As it turned out, the speaker that Sunday was Eric Gaudion who has suffered from an incredibly debilitating and painful disease for years, despite many prayers for healing. He spoke of that sense of failure and guilt that we can be tempted into when God does not seem to respond to our prayers. It felt as though he had been called in specifically to minister to me. How intimate, how personal, is life with God! Life so often flows like a warm conversation with our Creator, Father God! But at this point I did not know what was in store for me that evening.

That evening, sitting in our living room, I began to get increasingly breathless. After a while, despite heavy medication, this developed into the fiercest asthma attack I had ever experienced. For three-quarters of an hour it was like my head was tightly sealed in a plastic bag. My breathing was shallow and frantic. I was turning blue. I lost all control over my bodily functions and became certain I was going to die. I even wanted to die because I could imagine no other escape from this frightening state. I felt like I was in the midst of a desperate and dark battle over my life and I had nothing to fight with.

In my mind I cried out to God and the fear subsided somewhat, but the breathing didn't change. I was, however, sent a wonderful ambulance man. And then, unlike any attacks of the past, this one began to subside almost as quickly and unexpectedly as it had come. By the time I had arrived at the hospital, I could speak in full sentences and an hour or so later I was back to normal and discharged.

Amazingly, the whole episode had only begun four or five hours before but somehow it seemed like a lifetime ago. Our hearts were a cauldron of mixed and churning emotions – elation, relief, residual fear, celebration, vulnerability, awe and gratitude. It probably took a couple of days for the shock to work through our systems. During this time, we both came to realise that God had reached down and touched us that evening in a very special way – every bit as special as the healing experience four days previously. What may well have been an attack of the enemy, God had turned into a glorious victory in us both. We were changed people. There was a new depth of humility in our souls, a new depth of trust in Him and a new depth of love, both for Him and for each other.

Eric Gaudion, in his talk on healing, had shown how important it was to listen to God in these experiences and come to understand what he was saying through them. I had to admit I was pretty mystified. In less than one week I had nearly died from asthma and been miraculously healed of it . . . but in the wrong order! It was all just too inexplicable *not* to have an explanation! And, I did seek God for understanding. Eventually, I came to see that this was exactly what God *had* taught me through the experience.

It was as if God had said to me, 'Look, Kelvin, you have seen I have the power to take away your asthma in an instant. Your asthma is not bigger than me; I am far, far bigger than it. It is not something that has slipped out of my control, or that I have to struggle with in order to overcome. If it remains, that is simply because at present it is within my purposes and plans for you . . . which are always for your good and not for harm. Even if it were to accelerate to its most fierce, as you have seen, I will still be your fortress and it will not harm you. Your life is in *my* hands, my hands alone and the enemy will never snatch you from my grasp.'

This has been a wonderful and profound lesson for me and my heart overflows with gratitude and praise for the Father God who is so patient and deeply compassionate in his teaching.[56]

So God knows what he is doing, even if we don't. Psalm 147:4–5 says that God determines the number of the stars and calls them each by name, that he is great 'and mighty in power; his understanding has no limit'.

Knowing this we can perhaps enter in more fully to the attitude of early Christian believers who trusted God for the mysteries they could not understand and drew near to Christ so that they could receive all the revelation that God had made available to them in him. No wonder their hymnbook contained this remarkable song

> Oh, the depth of the riches of the wisdom and
>   knowledge of God!
> How unsearchable his judgments
> and his paths beyond tracing out!
> "Who has known the mind of the Lord?
> Or who has been his counsellor?"
> "Who has ever given to God, that God should repay
>   him?"
> For from him and through him and to him are all things.
> To him be the glory for ever! Amen (Rom. 11:33–36).

God is bigger than we think

Not only does God know full well what he is doing, but he is so much bigger than we think. Like the iceberg that hit and sank the *Titanic*, a huge part of God's nature and power are hidden from our view. We simply could not cope if we were able to see all of God, because his holiness, brilliance and power would overwhelm us. Job discovered this when he and his friends decided to challenge God to explain himself. Instead of answering their very understandable questions directly, God spoke to them and asked some pointed questions of his own, which had the effect of bringing a kind of hush from Job and his friends

> Where were you when I laid the earth's foundation?
> Tell me, if you understand.

Who marked off its dimensions? Surely you know!
Who stretched a measuring line across it?
On what were its footings set, or who laid its
    cornerstone –
while the morning stars sang together
and all the angels shouted for joy? (Job 38:4–7).

God is eternal and he is almighty and he is present everywhere. Sometimes I find it helpful to go outside at night
and think about how huge the universe is. Is there any
horizon or limit to it? Apparently light travels at three
hundred thousand kilometres per second. That's top
speed in this universe – nothing can go faster – but it's relatively slow compared to the distances to be travelled.
The nearest big galaxy to our Milky Way, the Andromeda
galaxy, is two million light-years away. The most distant
galaxies we can now see are ten or twelve billion light-
years away. We could never see a galaxy that is farther
away in light travel time than the universe is old – an esti-
mated fourteen billion or so years (give or take a few
years!). If that is so, then we are surrounded by a 'horizon'
that we cannot look beyond – a horizon set by the dis-
tance that light can travel over the age of the universe.

   This horizon describes the visible universe – a region
some 28 billion light years in diameter. But what would
be our horizon if we were standing on a planet at the very
limit of the visible universe, say one of the most distant
galaxies we see? And what if we could go and set up our
telescope on a planet in the galaxies at the limits of their
vision? There is every reason to think that the universe
extends a long way beyond the part of the universe we
can see. In fact, a variety of observations suggest that our
visible patch may be a small fraction – maybe an infin-
itely small fraction – of the whole. Yet God is there, everywhere present and what is more, he made it all. And this

is the God who calls us to trust him when the going gets hard for us. Yet all this power and 'Almightiness' would simply be scary and irrelevant to us in our adversity if we didn't also know that God loves us and cares about the most insignificant aspect of our lives.

God's love is deeper than we imagine

There is a poem and song written in French by Jean Richepin (1849–1926) which is called *La Chanson de Marie-des-Anges*. It has become the basis of folk-lore and poetry in Spanish, Portuguese and English, known as *The Ballad of the Speaking Heart* and is now a Celtic folk song. It tells the tale of a young man smitten by the love of a cruel woman, who demands the heart of his mother to feed her dog. The boy goes off to his house, attacks his mother and cuts out her heart (folk songs can get very gory). As he runs back to the lover with the heart in his hand he trips and falls, rolling down the steep incline, with the heart tumbling at his side. As he falls, he hears a voice coming from the heart asking 'Are you hurt my child? Are you hurt at all?'

At its finest and best, a mother's love is a mystery. What keeps her hanging on, believing the best for her offspring, caring intensely about their welfare and sacrificing so much for their success? Answer – a mother's love. And who invented, indeed created it? God did and it reflects his own care for his children. In fact, God's love for us vastly exceeds a mother's love. 'Can a mother forget the baby at her breast and have no compassion on the child she has borne? Though she may forget, I will not forget you!' is his promise to his children (Is. 49:15). Jesus himself expressed maternal sentiments in his lament over the sacred city: 'O Jerusalem, Jerusalem, you who kill the prophets and stone those sent to you, how often I have longed to gather your children together, as a hen gathers her chicks under her wings, but you were not willing' (Mt. 23:37).

Then the Father heart of God is also clear in the New Testament, especially in stories that Jesus told, such as The Prodigal Son which could be described as 'The Loving Father.' Reflecting on Rembrandt's magnificent painting of the return of the prodigal, Henri Nouwen says

> The parable of the prodigal son is a story that speaks about a love that existed before any rejection was possible and that will still be there after all rejections have taken place. It is the first and everlasting love of a God who is Father as well as Mother. It is the fountain of all true human love, even the most limited. Jesus' whole life and preaching had only one aim: to reveal this inexhaustible, unlimited motherly and fatherly love of his God and to show the way to let that love guide every part of our daily lives.[57]

What is amazing in this account of two young men – one of whom takes his father's wealth and squanders it on prostitutes and wild living in a far country, and the other who takes the same wealth and hordes it for selfish purposes at home – is how much love was in the father's heart for both his sons. He waited patiently for the return of the prodigal, watching from afar but not rushing in foolishly or prematurely to remove from him the consequences of his wrongdoing. When the boy came home, he also invited his other son to the celebration with a full tank of love for both of them. I find great help in that fact. Sometimes I feel like the younger prodigal son in the story and sometimes like the elder critical perfectionist brother. The father loved them both.

You matter to God

When dealing with adversity of all kinds, we will find our sense of self-worth running very low. Mine certainly does and I have spent long periods earnestly struggling to feel loved and valued despite how I see myself. Generally speaking I have been harder on myself than ever I needed to be. I am intolerant of my own mistakes, self-critical and imagine that I am a nuisance to those who love me or are serving me in one capacity or another. And then there have been those times of rebellion when I have gone my own way and done my own thing, for whatever reason. Returning to the loving Father and Mother of our souls is a vital part of rediscovering our sense of worth and knowing who we are in Christ. He loves us way beyond our understanding and much deeper than our failures and needs. In fact, I realise now that in all those years of trying to find God in order to feel more of his love, he was waiting all that time for me to be found by him.

An abiding memory I have is of being in Zimbabwe in very dangerous and difficult circumstances with our young son Matthew. I felt an overwhelming sense of concern for him and responsibility for his welfare. There is no way that I would have allowed him to fend for himself. And if that's how I love my child – and I'm a very imperfect father – how much more does God love me and care about the adversity that I am facing? Of course, it is not always easy to square that understanding of God's love with the way we feel that he has treated us. That is when we are called to trust in our heavenly Father and draw on the promises he has given us. Remembering what he told us in the light will keep us going in the dark.

When it was dark

Strangely, one of the darkest times in my life was not connected to my terrible illness or my time in hospitals. It was during the early period in our marriage. We were in the ministry and Matthew was not yet born, but Diane was suffering from dreadful clinical depression. There is something in men that makes us want to fix things and when I encountered this dark intruder in our marriage, I discovered that I was helpless – there was nothing I could fix. There came a time when I was forced to admit that this was not just Diane's problem – rather it was 'our problem'. Only then could I enter the counselling and prayer process that contributed so much to her recovery and she could find the help that she needed. Many times during those dreadful days, I called out to God saying 'Where are you?' and 'Why have you abandoned us?'

Calling out for help

Jesus used the same words on Good Friday. He cried out of the dereliction and distress of his heart 'My God, my God, why have you forsaken me?' (Mt. 27:46). We know that he was using the words of the psalmist from Psalm 22. His listeners around the cross would have known that too (at least the Jewish ones – the Greeks present thought that he was calling for Elijah). This fact has led some to suggest theories about why he spoke in this way. Maybe Jesus was using a well-prepared reference to the Old Testament so as to demonstrate that what he was going through had been foretold in the Scriptures? Perhaps he was calling to God out of a sense of disillusionment and defeat? I think that is unlikely in the light of all that Jesus taught about his death and resurrection in advance of the events. Maybe in quoting from the beginning of Psalm 22, Jesus was drawing the attention of his listeners (those who knew their Old Testament) to the teaching of the whole Psalm which includes great statements of victory at the end. And then there is another school of thought that explains that what Jesus was expressing was true – he had been forsaken by his Father because of the weight of sin that was laid upon him. John Stott sees it this way

> So then an actual and dreadful separation took place between the Father and the Son; it was voluntarily accepted by both the Father and the Son; it was due to our sins and their just reward; and Jesus expressed this horror of great darkness, this God-forsakenness, by quoting the only verse of Scripture which accurately described it and which he had perfectly fulfilled, namely; 'My God, my God, why have you forsaken me?'[58]

That last idea does it for me and what it means is that God the Son tasted total desolation and rejection. It was a genuine cry for help from a broken heart. It's not the sort of thing that prophets are supposed to say, let alone the Messiah. I find it immensely comforting to know that my Saviour prayed that way. When pain has driven me to a place where I felt I was losing my mind, when frustration with myself and my condition has made me want to tear my hair out, I remember that Jesus felt this way before me. At the centre of the storm that was going on at Calvary, Jesus could no longer feel his Father's presence. What he was doing that day is unique. I only feel abandoned, even though the Bible tells me that I am not. But he really was abandoned! His was desolation way beyond anything I will ever know. But for me, even the feeling of being left alone in my troubles is bad enough.

We live near the sea and watch it every day. When the sea is calm, 'like a millpond' as we say, you could drop a tiny pebble into it and you would see the ripples spread far. The sense of that encounter is immediately obvious; the evidence of the pebble's presence is easily recognised. When the sea is boisterous, however, especially in the thrashing and foaming chaos of storm force winds, you could heave in a boulder and you wouldn't even know where it had gone in. It would be there, but the signs of its entry would be swallowed up by the fierce nature of the storm. God's felt presence can be a bit like this. In times of calm and serenity we can occasionally 'feel' him near. When storm force winds are blowing, however, he may well be near in a big way but we can't perceive it. When I feel that way, I take comfort from the Saviour's prayer on the cross. His was not just a perceived God-forsakenness, it was real. He knows how I feel.

Chapter 13

Risen, Ascended, Glorified!

In the film *Cast Away*, the actor Tom Hanks plays FedEx employee, Chuck Noland, who is stranded on an uninhabited island after his plane goes down over the South Pacific. His family back home presume he is dead and hold a funeral for him, burying a weighted coffin in his name. Over four years later, following a dramatic mid-Pacific rescue, Chuck turns up at home to find his relatives absolutely aghast at the fact of his survival and return.

Yet the amazement that people would feel in such a situation pales into insignificance in the light of the experience of the first followers of Jesus Christ. They found themselves in the presence of one who was definitely and very publicly dead. Following the trauma of his execution and burial, Jesus walked to Emmaus with a couple of them and then sat at the table with them and broke bread (Lk. 24:13–31). He invited them to touch him (Jn. 20:27) and shared breakfast with them on the beach (Jn. 21:9–12). He appeared to more than five hundred of them at one time (1 Cor. 15:6).

Not surprisingly the resurrection became a major factor in the remarkable growth of the Early Church and its survival to this day. There were many religious sects in their day (the Greek cults of Zeus and Artemis, Jewish cults of the Pharisees, Sadducees etc.) yet none of them have survived the two millennia in any significant numbers, apart from the sect of the Nazarenes. The resurrection was the cornerstone of early preaching and teaching, the subject of their hymns and songs of victory. Along with the experience of being filled with the Holy Spirit at Pentecost, the resurrection of Jesus Christ was the driving force of first century missions. Daniel Clark, in his excellent book on the resurrection, says

> Within days of Jesus' death, all signs of grief were erased from the faces of Jesus' followers and within weeks, this tiny leaderless group had grown to number thousands – and they were voluntarily opposing the authorities, by now fearless of the possible consequences. It wasn't long before Stephen became the first Christian martyr, but far from damping down the spread of the movement, it only served to fan its growth out even further.[59]

This message of the resurrection did not only affect the preaching and spread of the Christian Church. It also became the cornerstone of their ability to endure pressure of all kinds. This is why Paul and his team were able to go through the immense pressure they experienced when they first entered the province of Asia (2 Cor. 1:8–9). They all felt that the great pressure was far beyond their ability to endure, causing them to despair even of life itself. Paul's recollection of this dark period is that 'this happened that we might not rely on ourselves but on God, who raises the dead.' In another letter to the same church, he reveals the key to enduring the most appalling suffering (1 Cor. 15:30–32). Having established in verse 20 that 'Christ has indeed been raised from the dead', Paul goes on 'And as for us, why do we endanger ourselves every hour? I die every day – I mean that, brothers – just as surely as I glory over you in Christ Jesus our Lord. If I fought wild beasts in Ephesus for merely human reasons, what have I gained? If the dead are not raised . . .'

Pain, suffering and even death do not have the final word. We are all 'terminal' as part of the human condition, but that is not the end of the story. If we are healed, we win! If we die, we win! Thanks to the resurrection of Jesus, life with its suffering is a win/win situation now for the Christian. Because Christ rose, we shall rise also. He is called the 'firstfruits' – like at harvest time – the token of an expected harvest. What happened to Jesus that first Easter will profoundly affect what happens to us when we die.

What happens when a believer dies?

My interest in what happens after death to someone who believes in Jesus is not academic for me. When I was first in hospital intensive care following the first attack of acute pancreatitis, I had two near-death experiences. Another was to follow after major surgery later that year. Since then I have gone down to theatre several times after being warned that there was a one in three risk of life-threatening complications involved in what the medical team were about to do to me. The condition that I suffer from has a high mortality rate. In addition, as a pastor, I have been with too many people at the moment of their passing or immediately afterwards, to be uninterested in what follows. So what does the Bible say happens to Christians at the moment of their death?

- Their spirit and soul go immediately to be with the Lord. We are not just flesh and blood. We are essentially a living soul consisting of our mind, intellect (including our emotions) and will. With our spirits, we communicate with God and have the ability to relate to him and to the spirit world. With our bodies, we relate to the physical world and interact with our environment. In Philippians 1:23 Paul confesses his desire 'to be with Christ which is better by far'. In 2 Corinthians 5:8 he describes the state of death for the believer as being 'away from the body and at home with the Lord'. This ties in with my own experience, described more fully in *Braving the Storm*, where when near death I felt that I was approaching a large wall and could hear glorious music from the other side. I heard a clear voice saying to me 'Not far now, Eric and Jesus will meet you there.' I know that place awaits me again in the future and I am not afraid of it.

- They are instantly in a conscious paradise. When Jesus was crucified, there were two thieves that died with him that day, one on either side. The one reviled him but the other, sobered by his sufferings and receiving insight into the true innocence of Jesus, asked the Lord to remember him when he came into his kingdom. His reply was 'I tell you the truth, today you will be with me in paradise' (Lk. 23:43). Paradise, then, is a 'today' thing at the point of death, not tomorrow or next year. In the Septuagint, the Greek version of the Old Testament, the meaning of the word translated here as 'paradise' was a garden (the Garden of Eden, Gen. 2:8–10) or a forest (Neh. 2:8). In the New Testament it means the place of bliss where believers join the angels in the worship of God and where the original fellowship between God and man that existed in Adam is restored (2 Cor. 12:2) along with access to the tree of life (Rev. 2:7).

- They await the future resurrection of the dead. This future event will occur at the end when Christ has defeated every enemy and power, especially the last enemy, death itself. Death is a common human condition (in Adam) but those who are in Christ will overcome the power of death (1 Cor. 15:52). Only then will we receive our resurrection bodies which will be like the risen body of Jesus. Then there will be a physical world without sin, pain, suffering, tears or death. This is the event that is symbolised in the Bible with language that speaks of the graves opening and the sea 'giving up her dead'. All this is far beyond our ability to understand and we are called to trust God and believe his promises. They are, however, confirmed by the historical resurrection of Jesus. Because he lives, we shall live also.

Pie now or in the sky?

The one aspect of this teaching, of course, that is hard to bear is the fact that it is all in the future. When you are in pain that drags on day after day, month after month and year following year, eternity can seem, well – an eternity away. Yet the writers of the New Testament, who lived in an era before antibiotics, anaesthesia and pain relief, longed for heaven with all their hearts and it did seem to bring them comfort. Despite the fact that they were blessed with healing miracles, they looked to the return of the Lord and the hope of heaven with eager expectation. In that sense they had their piece of pie now, not just in the sky. Can we learn from them?

Sandie is a dear friend of ours. She has been loyal and faithful in helping us all through the years of pain. She used to come into the intensive care unit with Diane and take my other hand and the two of them would pray over my unconscious body. But when we first grew to know her well, she had just lost her husband Mick, to cancer in his late thirties. She was left a young widow and their only child fatherless. Their marriage had been a real love match – a marriage made in heaven. When Mick died, Sandie was bereft, devastated. One aspect of her faith that took her through those terrible dark days and made it possible to receive us into her home and minister to us just months after his death, was her unshakeable expectation that she would see Mick again. Now that she is remarried and both Sandie and her second husband are pastors, she continues to have a strong interest in eschatology and the hope of heaven. It has seen her through the hard times, so she knows its worth.

> Therefore we do not lose heart. Though outwardly we are wasting away, yet inwardly we are being renewed day by day. For our light and momentary troubles are achieving for us an eternal glory that far outweighs them all. So we fix our eyes not on what is seen, but on what is unseen. For what is seen is temporary, but what is unseen is eternal (2 Cor. 4:16–18).

If you have been affected by any of the issues raised in this book, and would like to contact me, you may do so at my e-mail address

EricGaudion@hotmail.com

I would be pleased to hear from you. I would also be happy to come and speak to your group or church about these important matters.

Endnotes

1   Max Lucado, *Travelling Light* (Nashville: Word Publishing Group, 2001), p7.
2   M. David Enoch, *Healing the Hurt Mind* (London: Hodder & Stoughton, 1989), p14.
3   Rob Bell, *Velvet Elvis* (Grand Rapids: Zondervan, 2005), p30.
4   Ibid., p31.
5   Norman H. Snaith, *Distinctive Ideas of the Old Testament* (London: Epworth Press, 1950), p102.
6   Neil T. Anderson and Rich Miller, *Getting Anger Under Control* (Eugene: Harvest House Publishers, 2002), p84.
7   Andrew D. Lester, *Anger: Discovering your Spiritual Ally* (London: SPCK, 2007).
8   Steve Downes, 'Miracle Child' in *Christianity* magazine (August 2007).
9   Les Parrott III, *The Control Freak* (Wheaton: Tyndale House, 2000), p47.
10 Name has been changed to protect identity.
11 Corrie Ten Boom, *Reflections of God's Glory* (Grand Rapids: Zondervan, 1999), p25.
12 *The Secret Millionaire*, shown on Channel 4 on the 5th December 2007 at 2100hrs.
13 George Bernard Shaw, *Man and Superman* (London: Penguin, 2000), Epistle Dedicatory.

[14] John Stott, *The Cross of Christ* (Leicester: IVP, 1986), p245.

[15] Robert Dickinson, *God Does Heal Today* (Edinburgh: Rutherford House, 1995), p55.

[16] Kenneth Hagin Jnr., *Healing: Forever Settled* (Tulsa: Faith Library Publications, 2000), p2.

[17] Ibid., p4.

[18] David Petts, unpublished Ph.D. Thesis, *Healing and the Atonement* submitted to the University of Nottingham, 1993.

[19] Ray Hubbard, *Isaiah 53: Is There Healing in the Atonement?* (Bromley: New Life Press, 1972), p59.

[20] Keith Warrington, *Healing and Suffering* (Milton Keynes: Paternoster, 2005), p52.

[21] Assemblies of God Fundamental Truths 12, the Internet, A/G Online.USA, http://ag.org/top/Beliefs/Our_Message.cfm#Healing.

[22] Position Paper on 'Healing as an Integral Part of the Gospel' available at http://ag.org/top/Beliefs/Position_Papers/pp_4184_healing.cfm

[23] Colin Urquhart, *Receive Your Healing* (London: Hodder & Stoughton, 1993), p34.

[24] Dr T.J. McCrossan, *Bodily Healing and the Atonement*, eds. Dr Roy Hicks and Dr Kenneth E. Hagin (Tulsa: Faith Library Publications, 1982), foreword xvi.

[25] D.R. McConnell, *A Different Gospel: Biblical and Historical Insights into the Word of Faith Movement* (Peabody: Hendrickson, 1995).

[26] Peter H. Lawrence, *The Spirit Who Heals* (Eastbourne: Kingsway Publications, 2006), p187.

[27] David J. Bosch, *Transforming Mission* (New York: Orbis Books, 1996), p65.

[28] G. Eldon Ladd, *A Theology of the New Testament* (Guildford and London: Lutterworth Press, 1975), p69.

[29] Robert J. Hillman with Coral Chamberlain and Linda Harding, *Healing and Wholeness* (Carlisle: Regnum Books, 2002), p15.

[30] http://www.miraclevalley.net/subpage14.html.

[31] Alan Hugh McNeile, *The Gospel According to St Matthew*, Thornapple Commentaries (Grand Rapids: Baker Book House, 1980), p108.

[32] F.W. Beare, 'The First Epistle of Peter' (Oxford: Blackwell, 1961), p146.

[33] J. Ramsay Michaels, *Word Biblical Commentary, 49, 1 Peter* (Waco: Word Books, 1988), p135.

[34] Philip Greenslade, *1 Peter: Living Hope* (Farnham: CWR, 2004), p96.

[35] Ibid., p98.

[36] Gordon D. Fee, *The Disease of the Health and Wealth Gospels* (Beverly: Frontline Publishing, 1985), p20.

[37] Contained in 1 Corinthians 15:3.

[38] Gordon D. Fee, *The First Epistle to the Corinthians* (Grand Rapids: Eerdmans, 1987), p724.

[39] John Stott, *The Cross of Christ* (Leicester: IVP, 1986).

[40] Hubbard, p59.

[41] Stott, p245.

[42] Andrew Brandon, *Health and Wealth* (Eastbourne: Kingsway Publications, 1987), p64.

[43] Robert Dickinson, *Does God Heal Today* (Carlisle: Paternoster, 1995).

[44] Used by permission.

[45] Warrington, p41.

[46] Warrington, p33.

[47] Pete Greig, *God on Mute* (Eastbourne: Survivor, Kingsway, 2007), p214.

[48] John Wilkinson, *The Bible and Healing* (Edinburgh: The Handsel Press, 1998), p101.

[49] 'Footsteps in the Sand.' Generally believed to be author unknown. One version is attributed to Mary Stephenson 1936 (public domain).

[50] Editorial by Lyn Ramsay in *Contact*, the magazine of Central African Missions, 355 Blackpool Road, Preston, Lancs, PR2 3AB, England.

[51] Greig, p180.

[52] David Prior, *The Message of Joel, Micah and Habakkuk* in The Bible Speaks Today series (Leicester: IVP, 1998), p204.

[53] Taken from notes of the sermon made at the time.

[54] PMID: 8982961 [PubMed – indexed for MEDLINE]. Medical definition and survey results available on the Internet at http://www.ncbi.nlm.nih.gov/pubmed/8982961.

[55] Hillman, Chamberlain and Harding, p157.

[56] Used by permission.

[57] Henri J.M. Nouwen, *The Return of the Prodigal Son* (London: Darton Longman and Todd, 1994), p108.

[58] Stott, p81.

[59] Daniel Clark, *Dead or Alive?* (Nottingham: IVP, 2007), p134.